Of Landscape and Longing

Anthologies edited by Carolyn Servid

The Book of the Tongass
coedited with Donald Snow

From the Island's Edge: A Sitka Reader

Of Landscape and Longing

Finding a Home at the Water's Edge

Carolyn Servid

MILKWEED EDITIONS

The names of a few people who appear in this book have been changed.

Published 2000 by Milkweed Editions
Printed in the United States of America
Cover design by Tara Christopherson, Fruitful Results Design
Cover painting by Julie Genz
Interior design by Donna Burch
The text of this book is set in Apollo, Joanna, and New Baskerville.
00 01 02 03 04   5 4 3 2 1
First Edition

Milkweed Editions, a nonprofit publisher, gratefully acknowledges support from our
World As Home funders: Lila Wallace-Reader's Digest Fund; Creation and Presentation
programs of the National Endowment for the Arts; and Reader's Legacy underwriter,
Elly Sturgis. Other support has been provided by the Elmer L. and Eleanor J. Andersen
Foundation; James Ford Bell Foundation; Bush Foundation; Target Foundation on
behalf of Dayton's, Mervyn's California and Target Stores; General Mills Foundation;
Honeywell Foundation; Jerome Foundation; McKnight Foundation; Minnesota State
Arts Board through an appropriation by the Minnesota State Legislature; Norwest
Foundation on behalf of Norwest Bank Minnesota; Lawrence and Elizabeth Ann
O'Shaughnessy Charitable Income Trust in honor of Lawrence M. O'Shaughnessy;
Oswald Family Foundation; Ritz Foundation on behalf of Mr. and Mrs. E. J. Phelps Jr.;
John and Beverly Rollwagen Fund of the Minneapolis Foundation; St. Paul Companies,
Inc.; Star Tribune Foundation; U.S. Bancorp Piper Jaffray Foundation on behalf of
U.S. Bancorp Piper Jaffray; and generous individuals.

Library of Congress Cataloging-in-Publication Data

Servid, Carolyn.
    Of landscape and longing : finding a home at the water's edge / Carolyn Servid.
    —1st ed.
    p.   cm.
    ISBN 1-57131-238-2 (pbk.)
    1. Servid, Carolyn.   2. Sitka Region (Alaska)—Description and travel.
  3. Landscape—Alaska—Sitka Region.   4. Sitka Region (Alaska)—Biography. I. Title.
F914.S6 S47 2000
979.8′2—dc21   99-046482

For my parents, Lester and Harriet Servid

Of Landscape and Longing

Of Landscape and Longing

Introduction

Outside the windows of our house is a crowded landscape, a typical one for Southeast Alaska, thick forests hug-
ging hillsides that rise steeply from rocky shorelines to the
alpine limits of the craggy mountains that are squeezed
into the confines of Baranof Island. There is no open level
ground within view, and there is not much within any
proximity. Everything gives way to slope and most slopes
are covered with dense trees. The sense of space here is
created by water, the bays, inlets, coves, and open channels where the North Pacific Ocean moves in to fill geological voids carved in the land. Fractures and rifts and
chasms that cut deep into this massif of rock and earth
create a convoluted shoreline. Still, there are stretches
along the island's edge where the land slopes more gently
to meet the water and offers a perch for a house like ours
and a bench big enough for a town like Sitka. As the tide
rises and falls—as much as sixteen feet—both the land and
those spaces across water shrink and swell accordingly.
The predominant orientation here is toward that open
watery space with the island's steep slopes at our backs.

Our house falls into suit. Its front corner of windows

faces due south and looks out over Thimbleberry Bay and beyond into Eastern Channel, a prominent east-west passage out to open ocean. It is tucked into a hillside, a sheltering stand of cedar, hemlock, and Sitka spruce, and is rimmed by a profusion of red huckleberry. The land in front of the house falls away to a rocky beach thirty feet below. The trees and berry bushes push toward the water's edge, putting down roots wherever they can find a bit of soil. Eventually they give way to the tidal zone and the barnacled rocks that are washed by remnants of ocean swells or waves kicked up by a breeze. Behind the house, the trees climb a hill that continues steeply skyward to terminate in the triangular rock summit of Mount Verstovia, three thousand feet above the water. The road into town cuts across its extended slope a hundred feet above our house, and we make our way to it each day by way of a quarter-mile trail that meanders through the trees. Standing on the beach rocks with my rubber-booted feet in the water, I sometimes try to place myself in that range—the sea floor falling away beyond me, the barnacles underfoot, the huckleberry just above me, the trees towering above those bushes, the shoulder of the mountain looming toward the clouds, and that stone summit soaring over all. The small stretch of rocky beach is one of the few natural open spaces between the water of Thimbleberry Bay and the high rock that crowns Verstovia's sharp rise. I pick my way cautiously, tentatively over the broken shoreline to a little ledge in a sloping face of stone where I can sit. Then I ease myself down, lean my small back against the mountain, and try to soak up some of its certainty.

A few feet from where I sit, that seaward sweep begins, the coastal deep that breaks up this compact, sharp-crested, forested land. The watery expanse limits my wanderings, but at the same time its openness gives me breathing room. A reaching finger of ocean separates me from a contiguous part of the island, from the spiky summits of the Pyramids and the rounded ridges of Mount Longenbaugh across the way. The enclave of Thimbleberry Bay is somewhat protected by the Marshall Islands a half mile out, but just beyond them Eastern Channel offers a straight shot at the North Pacific. That oceanic horizon, not quite in view, extends itself over a third of the globe to the shorelines of Siberia and Japan and China. Baranof Island hangs on the Pacific's eastern rim, its own complex piece in the three-hundred-mile straggle of islands that shape this northern coast. Here on its western edge, this rock, this beach, this forest, this slope are my vantage points. I am grounded here with the mountain against my back. This island's edge is home.

The Distance Home

The mirror of my childhood reflects a distant world that I shelter against its diminished place in time. There is a small two-room house for a family of seven, the home of my earliest playmates, no running water or electricity, the floors and built-in porch seats smoothed with a dried-hard coating of watered-down cow dung. There is a five- or six-year-old girl with sandy blond braids amidst a group of dark-skinned Indian children, sitting cross-legged on a stone schoolroom floor, writing the hanging letters of the Marathi language with a hard chalk pencil on her own small wood-framed slate. The same young girl is carrying a black umbrella, walking in a warm monsoon downpour, deliberately hitting all the puddles in order to break in a new pair of *chappals,* leather sandals that the cobbler at the little open shop at the *nakah,* the corner market, had just finished for her. The same young girl warily eyes lepers with grossly deformed limbs making their way haltingly toward the mission hospital gate. She spends idle time on an upstairs veranda, watching the traffic go by on the road beyond a garden wall—bony cows hooked up to wooden carts hauling loads to the bazaar; thin dark barefoot women, bright-colored saris pulled up between their legs, carrying stacked jugs of water on their heads; men dressed in baggy white clothes against the heat, stopping and turning their backs to the road to urinate in the ditch; only an occasional vehicle, maybe a lorry or a battered blue-and-yellow state transport bus, the people inside looking out from under the rolled-up canvas flaps above the glassless windows. And then the same young girl, a year or two later, gets on one of those buses with her brother and two sisters, and then on a train with twenty other children, a couple of chaperones, and a throng of Indian people to make the three-day journey to a boarding school seven hundred fifty miles away from home.

Or maybe it was twelve thousand miles away from home if you consider that we were an American family living in a small coastal village in western India, Vengurla, a place where we didn't really belong. Not that we weren't welcomed and appreciated at the Presbyterian mission hospital there. We were. And not that we weren't comfortable. We lived in an ample house, had a cook, a woman who cleaned for us, and an ayah who took care of us as young children. But our time in India was grounded in the assumption that at some point we would return *home*. Back then *home* was a nebulous place in California or Washington, near one of the spots my parents knew from their own childhoods and college years. *Home* would never finally be Vengurla, even after twelve years there, even for me, though that warm air afforded me my first breath, though it was the first place on earth I came to love.

Few of us live out our lives in the place we were born, but there, on the far side of our earliest memories, are the details of the earth's embrace that first gave us ground. Before the Marathi and English words and letters were sorting themselves out in my mind, before the playmates, before my first very own school slate, there was the iron red dirt, the shimmer of tropical light, the shade of the mango tree in our backyard, the electric green of wet rice fields, a warm white sand beach and the cerulean blue expanse of the Arabian Sea. There were the cries of crows, the monsoon thunder, the steam rising off thatched roofs and dirt and pavement after the rain. There were the kind words of Indian nurses and doctors, maintenance workers and church members who helped me learn their language, let me move among them with ease. They would never have said I didn't belong there.

But in spite of their kindness, in spite of the affections they nurtured in me, I had to grow into the fact that I was not one of them. I was undeservedly privileged. I lived in the big house. My father was the hospital superintendent, my mother the head technician in the lab. We were Americans. We always had the option of an escape from India's discomforts—from poverty and disease, the disarray and inconveniences of an underdeveloped country. My parents knew and relied on this. At the time, I didn't.

Every five years we escaped for a year's leave of absence *at home*—somewhere on the American west coast. For me, those were trips to a foreign country. Riding school buses, strolling bountiful grocery store aisles with my mother, driving wide highways in comfortable cars, talking on the telephone, perhaps most of all watching television. We weren't allowed much TV time, and little of what I saw stayed with me, but I looked forward to game shows like *Concentration,* where I could pit my own wit against the contestants, first remembering where the pairs of numbers lay, then puzzling out the sentence or phrase that the hidden pictures and letters gradually revealed. And I remember *Queen for a Day,* the chance for lucky weeping housewives to be showered with the apparel and furnishings and fixtures that constituted some notion of the American woman's dream. I watched without knowing that my young fantasies played straight into the hand of materialism and presumption.

But America was a world apart. When we returned to India, life picked up where I'd left it—the barefoot days in the red dirt between the coconut palms, on the cool floors under high whitewashed walls and ceilings, on the dung-smoothed little courtyard in front of Irikini's house. She was our housekeeper; her daughters Jammu and Bashu were my earliest friends. They welcomed me in their two-room home, shared their fresh warm *chapatis.* We gathered jasmine blossoms and sat together on their small porch making fragrant flower chains for our hair. I never thought of telling them about those television game shows. Somehow, my young mind understood that there was no context in their lives for that contrived reality. And now, over the years of distance, I let my memory sway with the motion of Irikini working in our big house, the swish of her wet rag as she swept it in repeated arcs back and forth across the red tile floor. I remember her thin legs, squat-walking from one end of a room to the other. I remember her plain green cotton sari neatly tucked up to give her room to work, her black oiled hair pulled back from her handsome face into a coiled knot on the back of her head, her shy smile, fingers at her mouth to cover her large straight teeth. Irikini would never be queen for a day, but when I put her image beside my recollections of those thrilled American housewives surrounded by new wardrobes and jewelry and furniture and appliances, she is the one who comes out shining.

My affections for Vengurla afforded me my first experiences of homesickness—that longing for what was familiar, for people with whom I felt safe, for a place where I could be myself and felt I belonged. Irikini's front porch was one of those places—compact, protected, with niche-like seats and benches that collected people in a comforting way, its single step leading down into the small courtyard framed on one side by a building, on the other by a row of thin trees. Another was our own house's long veranda, which ran the second-story length of the bungalow. The rooms inside were big and high-ceilinged, airy and cool. But the porch was our playground while our parents were at work. My sisters and brother and I would sit in a circle with Ayah or Irikini and play Marathi hand games, a nonsense rhyme about chickens and eggs and blue horses and frogs setting us in motion, absorbing us in laughter:

Ugulal, mugulal, thal thulwar
kombadichi gulwar, kombadichi unda
bil bil gonda, chikini supari
nila gorda, dhudum dhudki
sugundhachi bedki.

We spent hours creating worlds of circumstance with the set of wooden blocks made by Sawla, the hospital carpenter—forts and houses and towers occupied by people and plots of all kinds. We'd throw a spread of jacks across the tile floor and pick them up in pairs or threes or sixes, each sweep with one bounce of the ball. From the west end of the porch we could look out over the rolled-dirt tennis court and watch late afternoon games between the hospital staff, giggling our own comments about one very serious fellow whose stiffly pressed culottes matched the style of his serve.

Off the front of the porch, an open concrete *agasha* extended out to create a portal over the driveway that bordered the circle of garden and brought an occasional car to a stop at the front door. It was another courtyard, an elevated lookout over the roses and gardenias and jasmine bushes and beyond the garden wall to the road that was the main byway in and out of Vengurla. The *agasha's* cement collected moss, and its heavy balusters were a gathering spot for raucous crows that woke me in the mornings. From here we could see the tropical night skies. My father took us out there when he woke us in

the dark early hours to look at the Southern Cross. And
the *agasha* was the best place for a five- or six-year-old
like me to stand in my underwear in a warm monsoon
downpour, delighting in the shower of water on my head
and shoulders, belly and back, breathing in the musty
sweetness that rose from the hot wet pavement and dirt.

No memory of Vengurla finds its way out of my mind
without going first to that west Indian coast — the beach
we returned to again and again, up and over the dune
with its palms, then down the long sloping stretch of
open white sand, past the Hindu temple inside its own
stone wall, sheltered by its own groves of green, to
the edge of tumbling warm water, blue and green and
frothy white. Occasionally we shared that stretch of
waterfront with a few Indian fishermen, but more often
we had it to ourselves for hours of swimming and bask-
ing in the sun, a singularly un-Indian pastime. Leaving
our towels and *chappals* and extra clothes on the sand,
we would give in almost immediately to the refreshing
lure of the ocean. My mother could tread water in a
seated position forever, it seemed, and would let me
climb in her lap and ride the swells. I learned how to
dive off my father's shoulders. Sometimes I lay on my
back and floated over the waves out beyond where I
could touch bottom, content with the water's undulations and the broad reach of sky. When I put my feet
down and didn't find ground, I'd swim back toward
shore. If I was lucky, I'd catch a wave as it broke and ride
it all the way in until it delivered me on my belly in the
beach sand. When I tired of the surf, I was content on

shore, collecting cuttlebone and shells with delicate zig-zag lines or brush-stroke patterns that could have come off a Chinese calligrapher's pen. On the special occasions when we took a picnic dinner to the beach, we stared into the sunset waiting for the elusive green flash that sometimes edges the sun just as it disappears below the horizon. When we didn't see it, we settled for the phosphorescence that lit up the breaking waves and coated our bodies as we moved through the water. Off on the horizon the recurring flash of a lighthouse measured the night and an occasional ship strung with lights passed us by. When we finally headed home I would suck the briny water out of the ends of my braids and put in my dibs for a turn in the smooth concrete wash-tubs on the back porch where I could rinse off the day's salt and sand.

Homesick, we say, when our hearts reach back to those places that have embraced us, our language allowing us the truth that when we are away from them we feel unhealthy, ill at ease. *Sentimentality,* another voice says, urging me to ignore the bonds that form between the human heart and particularities of the earth. But perhaps the sentiments we attach to place are more natural to us than we know. Perhaps what is at work is an instinctual desire, a need, for a set of specific details to help determine our bounds, our own habitat, a particular context within which we can come to know how best to live our individual lives, how best to survive not only within the human community, but in a distinct region of the larger natural community that is our only true home.

"Consider one born in the desert," says poet Pattiann Rogers,

> How he must see his sorrow rise
> In the semblance of the yucca spreading
> Its thorn-covered leaves in every direction,
> Pricking clear to the ends
> Of his fingers. He recognizes it
> And deals with it thus.
> . . . .
> And consider the child raised near the sea, impinged
> Upon constantly by the surf rising in swells,
> Breaking itself to permanent particles of mist
> Over the cliffs. Did you really think
> The constant commotion of all that fury
> Would mean nothing in the formation of the vocabulary
> Which he chooses to assign to God?

When I was seven, I went off to boarding school for nine months of the year, and Vengurla became the place I was from rather than where I lived. My new home away from home was the seven thousand-foot-high spot of Kodaikanal, a Tamil town in the Palni Hills, a small mountain range near the southern tip of India. The British were the first foreigners to capitalize on Kodai's assets as an escape from the tropical heat ten degrees north of the equator. They established a hill station there in 1845. Over time they made it comfortable for themselves—dammed up a stream to create an enchanting lake, built a road around its three-mile circumference that curved in and out along a wooded shore, set up a boat club so they could use the lake whenever they pleased in their leisure time, and organized a retinue of Indian people to cater to them. They laid the groundwork that made Kodai a prime site for the school that was founded in 1901 for children of the next waves of foreigners. By the time I began attending in the 1960s, there were almost four hundred elementary-through-high-school students enrolled, and Kodai School was a fixed part of the Indian community's economy. Its compound on the hillside above the lake was a central part of the town.

My new cohorts and roommates, fellow missionary children, were from other coastal and central parts of the Indian subcontinent, regions that their Lutheran or Baptist or Methodist church mission boards had staked out. I couldn't imagine that any of those places was as beautiful as Vengurla. My biases didn't matter, though. What we had in common was a sense of uprootedness. Our fundamental connections to family and home were all changed. My brother and sisters were at school with me, but they were in different dorms and I had to get permission to visit them. A whole group of new adults—houseparents, teachers, and administrators—was there to stand in for my parents, who I would continue to know primarily through weekly letters. And Kodai didn't smell of steamy dust or the ocean. Its high-altitude air cooled off to a sweater chill. The trees were eucalyptus, not palm and mango. The steep terrain fell away thousands of feet in places to open up a vista over the expanse of the hot hazy Indian plain. To my young mind, it almost seemed as though I should be able to see my way home.

Instead, the confines of the school grounds provided some small reassurance in the definition they offered this new life—my own place in Upper Boyer Hall, one of the girls' dorms on the far side of the compound from the boys' dorms. The classroom complex, dining hall, library, and gym were spread out on the hill between the dorms. And though I was eager to go to Kodai because I thought it meant I was grown up, those initial weeks, maybe months, were a blur of uncertainty. My new friends and I consoled ourselves by putting out our favorite possessions or photographs or by continuing familiar habits that helped ease our vulnerability. My first roommate had a clock that sat on her dresser, its face decorated with an American barnyard scene and a moving chicken that pecked at the tidy ground in sync with the clock's loud ticking. At night she would hush it by putting it under a stack of sweaters in a bottom drawer, faithfully getting it back out each morning. But I more than made up for her muffled clock. Nothing was more comforting to me in that strange dark room than to rock from side to side in my bed and sing myself to sleep—sometimes a distinct song, but more often just a low chant to match the cadence of my rocking. I don't remember that my roommate complained, at least not directly to me. I do know that I was the talk of that end of the dormitory hall. Everyone could hear me. Our housemother would sometimes come in and try a soothing hand on my shoulder. But I didn't know any other way to ease myself into those long lonely hours. If I lay still, the night was too big around me. There was too much room for the empty ache of homesickness, remembering the warm nights in that high-ceilinged bedroom in Vengurla, the certainty of knowing my parents were downstairs reading by the soft light of the living-room lamps, easing out of their day with the phonograph turned down low, the strains of classical violin or piano floating up the stairs, intermingling with my own music-in-sway. I didn't realize that I might never feel that safe again.

The Kodai school year broke in October for a three-month vacation that allowed us to return home for the Christmas and New Year holidays. I remember the excited sleepless night before our early morning departure, the twenty or thirty of us Presbyterian kids who traveled to-gether with a couple of chaperones to our western region of the country. Those were three-day journeys of antici-pation, first fifty miles down the Kodai *ghat* to catch the train, then a clackety rhythmic swaying ride halfway up India's triangle, each yellow-and-black railway station sign counting down the miles and hours—Tiruchchirappalli, Erode, Bangalore, Tumkur, Davangere, Hubli, Dharwar. Finally, at Belgaum, Mom met our family foursome, and we left the rest of the school party to make our final bus connection to Vengurla. That last leg took us down another *ghat* off the Deccan plateau to the Konkan coast. The breeze coming in under the bus' canvas window flaps began to have some moisture in it, and as the dirt got redder and the palm trees more frequent, it was harder and harder to be anything but happy. At last the old blue-and-yellow state transport rolled past our garden wall and slowed to a stop in front of one of the hospital compound gates. We piled off into the arms of Dad and other welcomers while someone climbed on top of the bus to get our luggage. And there was our roomy house with its *agasha* and garden, the tennis court, the mango tree. Irikini and Jammu and Bashu were waiting. Roki, our cook, had fixed a special dinner. The familiar came back in waves of simple joy. I was home.

"A sense of place is a primary category of faith," suggests theologian and historian Walter Brueggemann. Rootedness in place provides an essential context and coherence that allows us to know who we are by way of where we are, that allows us to act, to move our lives into their own significance. As a child, I intuitively came by a naive version of that faith, absorbing the details of place by a kind of sensory and emotional osmosis. The smell of fresh rain dampening the dry hot dirt let me come to a simple-hearted belief in renewal. The ocean's enticing waves, the myriad curiosities in the sand, were again and again a source of delight and possibility. The same air that prickled my skin with heat rash was a soft comfort on warm evenings. The same skies that were unbearably clear on the hottest days were full of starry wonder at night. Irikini and her family, our cook, Roki, and the hospital staff were people whose loyalties would never pale. That earliest faith was perfect in its innocence, holy in its implicit trust. I couldn't imagine that it was incomplete, that it wouldn't last. In all my comings and goings from Vengurla during the years we lived there, for boarding school or family furloughs to the States, those early certainties held ground. They still do—out of context as they now are—through the bonds that memory and love allow.

On my refrigerator, in the home I have found in Southeast Alaska, half a planet and lifetime away from Vengurla, is a photograph of Irikini and my mother. They are standing together with a group of people—Irikini's sister, a nephew, one of her daughters, and three other young women. My mother is wearing a green-and-black checked sari, a black sari blouse, and her *mangal sutra,* a necklace of black beads and gold traditionally worn by married women. Irikini's sari is white with a lavender pattern in it, a soft cotton sari that she has wrapped around both shoulders like a comforting shawl. My mother has her arm around Irikini's thin waist. They are smiling, my mother's a self-conscious but confident smile, Irikini's a shy close-mouthed one. Behind them is the house where Irikini now lives, thatched palm awnings shading the door, the large leaves of banana trees beyond. My father took the picture when he and my mother returned to Vengurla for a visit in 1986. I try to imagine Irikini in a house other than the tiny one where she welcomed me. I wonder if she has a bed to sleep on rather than a mat she rolls out on the floor. I wonder if her kitchen has a stove rather than a molded earthen fire niche in a corner.

I knew from my own return visit in 1973 that my memories had to make room for change. My childhood world had shrunk. In adult proportions, the hospital compound was compact—the buildings smaller and everything closer together than I remembered. The big house where we'd lived had been altered. An outside set of stairs helped turn the second floor into a separate dwelling, guest quarters where I stayed with my two traveling companions. Part of the upstairs veranda had been closed in, and the *agasha*—still there with the gardens below it— served as a second-story front porch. The road beyond the garden wall seemed barely wide enough for more than one lane of traffic.

When word got to Irikini that I had arrived, she came quickly up the new stairs to the *agasha,* tears streaming down her smiling face. We wept in each other's arms until our joy turned to laughter. That afternoon I sat with her and Jammu and Bashu on the little dung-coated porch seats of their two-room house. They were full of stories and questions and news, and I could feel the lilt of their spoken Marathi wake a flush of buried memories, words and their meanings clicking back into place, language synapses reuniting like long-lost companions. My unpracticed native tongue bumped along the edges of the conversation while I basked in the familiar sounds and meter. It didn't matter that I didn't understand it all. I listened while they combed my hair and adorned it with flowers, the blooms' sweetness mingling with the light scent of the oil in their combs. That night or the next— the memories swim together in time—Irikini insisted on fixing dinner for me and my fellow travelers, long-time family friends who were missionaries at an inland Presbyterian hospital. They used to visit us in Vengurla when we lived there, idled away days with us at the beach. Irikini hardly knew them. Still she honored us all. She splurged to buy meat for the curry, fixed steamy basmati rice, vegetables, *koshambir,* and *pooris*—a meal more elaborate than any she could afford for herself and her family. She had spread colorful *satrangis* on the floor in the main room of the house where we would sit and had set out enough places for the three of us and her husband, Paulu. Like a proper Indian hostess, she served us our food, then retreated to the kitchen and refused to eat with us.

I don't remember the dinner conversation, but my discomfort that evening still makes me wince. I was heartbroken. The dinner was delicious, but it was all wrong. I ached to be there alone with Irikini and her family, gathered around her kitchen cooking fire, all of us, sitting cross-legged on the dung-smoothed floor as we used to do, eating plain old *chapatis* or simple *pez,* the watery rice she would never serve to guests because it was common fare. I longed to erase the inequalities that separated us that evening, to know what I might do to honor her.

I don't remember our good-byes at the end of that

visit. I don't remember our earlier good-byes each time I left to go to Kodai for school. Perhaps I never wanted to acknowledge our parting, never knew how to face the difference in our lives—mine with its privilege, Irikini's with its quiet acquiescence to circumstance. Across the distance and years, I study that photograph, concentrate on her face, smile back at those eyes smiling out of the past at me.

Sometime in that Vengurla visit, Jammu agreed to take me to the bazaar so I could buy some *bangardis,* the thin colored glass bracelets that Indian women like to wear. The bangardi wallah's stall glittered with reds and greens, blues and lavenders, flashes of gold, column upon column of bangles stacked neatly on cardboard tubes, lining the walls behind him. He took my hand to gauge the size. What color? *Nila,* we decided. Blue ones to start with. He brought down a selection off his wall, then systematically checked them for cracks. Holding six or eight at a time, his fingers and thumb around the outside diameter, he quickly squeezed each bangardi until it popped down to hang on his thumb. Occasionally a cracked one broke in his hand. He brushed the pieces away and kept on, the measured tinkling of glass sprinkling through the clamor of the bazaar. When he was satisfied with his sampling, he took my hand again, folded it in on itself, and gently squeezed some *bangardis* over my knuckles and onto my wrist. If they were too big, I would bang them against

things and break them more easily. First the blue, pale
glass with a darker stripe inside and flecks of gold paint
in little paired notches spaced evenly around the outside
of each bangle. *Atcha.* They were just the right size. Then
a plain dusky rose faceted all the way around the outer
edge. Then lavender glass with three thin stripes inside
and a pattern of triple notches spaced half an inch apart.
They were all delicate and lovely. My wrists danced inside
them. Their music accompanied every motion. Jammu
smiled approval. I bought a dozen of each for a few ru-
pees. When I wore them, they would let Vengurla rever-
berate through whatever air surrounded me.

And sometime during that visit, my friends and I went
to the beach. I thought I would remember the way there
but couldn't quite. Still, we found the place to cut between
the small yards and houses lined up along the red-dirt
edge of solid ground that meets the sand and walked out
to the dunes. They were small hills, not the high slopes
I remembered. The waves rolled in over a much closer
shore. It was monsoon season and the water churned in
an irregular pattern of murky tumbling chop, not the
welcoming blue sea and long smooth breakers that used
to call to me. I had never seen the tempestuous face of
this ocean, had never imagined it wasn't always a safe
place to swim. As we walked along the beach, our conversation gave way to the steady thunder of surf coming
ashore. I took deep breaths of the tangy salt air and wandered over the wet sand looking for shells, the small clam-
shaped ones with their delicate patterns. They weren't
there. Surely they must be, I thought, but found no sign.

On some unexplainable impulse I started digging, and there, five or six inches down I uncovered a layer of them, their perfection a kind of buried treasure. One cream with thin yellow zigzag stripes, two white with soft brown bamboolike brush strokes, another smaller one, just a half inch wide, striped lavender with the contours of its form and painted with tiny V-shaped lines. I took these to the water's edge, washed them, and put them carefully in a close pocket, a stay against their disappearance, a gesture to keep the first place I loved from completely slipping away.

I have yet to understand all the ways in which that tropical village can be meaningful to me these many years later, but its place in the treasury of remembrance is steadfast. Its light and warmth, the ripe fragrance of its fruits and flowers, the rust red earth skirting the green of palms and rice fields, the turquoise water tumbling over white sands were all primary truths—first realities, first intimacies, first inklings of the meaning of my life. What became woven between and behind and around them was the other primary truth that anchored an early ache of longing in an uncomprehending young heart. I could not call this place *home;* this was not where I belonged. For years I sidestepped that unsettling. I distracted myself with adolescence, lost sight of those early bearings after our move to the United States in the sixties. For years I ignored the human hunger that Brueggemann recognizes for a sense of place. But Vengurla has come back to me time and again as a reminder—that the colors and smells and textures, the landscape, the people who belong to a place can elicit a love that is as sure as any we are likely to find on this earth.

Miss Burke

Miss Burke's door was the last one on the right at the end of the hall, a dark wood double door, thin enough that if you put your ear against it, you could guess at what might be happening on the other side. I envision a knocker on it, though I'm not certain the knocker was there. I remember the door more clearly than I remember the apartment inside. That entrance was a point of permission and approval, an opening to adult reassurances about the world. As a young girl, I stood in front of the door many times, often in fear, afraid the approval and reassurances would be withheld. Miss Burke was housemother for twenty-five or thirty adolescent girls who lived in Lower Boyer Hall at Kodaikanal School, an interdenominational Christian boarding school for children of missionary families in India. She oversaw not only our general well-being, but that of our souls. She was stewardess of the faith we were expected to embrace as part of our families' foreign endeavors.

The boarding school's routines were familiar to me by the time I came under Miss Burke's care. I'd been through several school terms and knew about rising bells, class schedules, dining-hall rules, laundry day, and weekend rest hours when we cleaned our rooms and wrote letters home. I did my best to keep my name off the posted list of people who had earned black marks for one sort of misconduct or another and had to serve detention when the marks piled up into full-fledged demerits. And I obediently took part in evening devotions, which Miss Burke added to our weekly schedule. All of Lower Boyer Hall would gather in her apartment for readings and prayers, sometimes a shared and silent group prayer where private concern or regret would build until it spilled off our tongues out into the open, into the expectation of compliance and confession.

Besides our visits to Miss Burke for devotions, we would go to her individually, too. There were simple questions—about our allowance or going off the school compound for a few hours—for which we could drop by. For discussions that were checks on the development of our faith, we were expected to schedule appointments. Those were some of the first appointments I made in my life. I would knock timidly at Miss Burke's door, already afraid of my guilt, and wait out those long moments with my heart literally pounding in my ears. That thin door would open to her sturdy skirted figure, her short dark wavy hair rounding out her face, her glasses lending an appropriate air of authority. She would welcome me with a matronly smile, then shut the door behind me and close out the rest of the world.

We would sit close, in chairs facing each other, and I would recite Bible verses I had memorized as a demonstration of what I had learned and what I thought I should believe. "John 3:16: For God so loved the world that He gave his only begotten Son that whosoever believeth in Him should not perish, but have everlasting life." I had a good memory, so the recitation was easy. The questions that followed put knots in my throat. Did I truly believe? Had I let Jesus into my heart? My trembling conscience would try then and there to open up some spot inside my chest and feel something flow in. I couldn't possibly say no. A no would cast me in the lot of sinners. I would be a problem. My parents might hear about it, and my father had once told me, when I was impatient with his reading of scripture, never to turn my back on God's word. But how could I know for sure that Jesus was within? And what did it really mean? Was it enough for me just to *think* that He was there, in my racing heart? Miss Burke was waiting. My whole life seemed caught in those few seconds of uncertainty. I was too vulnerable to dare a doubt, compliant and afraid. I knew that it was a matter of just one word. "Yes," I would say timidly, and a wave of relief would sweep into my gaping heart. Miss Burke would smile and sit with me for a minute, then go to a cupboard and come back with a Cadbury's chocolate bar or a package of Juicy Fruit gum. I always took those sweet reassurances back to my room and put them in my lock-drawer where I could be certain they were both safe and mine. When I savored them later, one piece at a time, whatever link they might have had between the Holy Spirit and my fearful faith got lost in their sugary succulence.

Thinking about it now, I imagine Miss Burke assumed

her charge was to firmly anchor our young minds in values she trusted would provide us a good life. Kodai School was a temporary staging ground. We were a generation coming of age in a country that was not our own, in a place that was not our home, among people who were not family. Our community was a little Anglo-American enclave catered to by the Indians of the town who must have appreciated the economic advantages we offered more than the spiritual benefits of our religious colonialism. We were protected from the press of India's ordinary life—people crowded together, people eking out a living, people hungry, people disfigured by disease, people segregated by a caste system that defied our American notion of equality. I remember unclearly a brief academic introduction to classic works of Indian literature, to Hindu traditions and spiritual beliefs. Something more thorough might have challenged the sense of values that teachers and staff, Miss Burke among them, worked diligently to establish. If anything could provide stable ground in the midst of this uprooted existence, they felt it would be the certainty of strong Christian beliefs. For them, the vulnerability of young questioning minds posed the perfect opportunity to cultivate faith; if that faith could take hold early, there was a chance it might last.

On Sundays, Miss Burke would see to it that we joined the rest of the school at services in the chapel. Compared to the blurred memory of the interior of her apartment, my recollections of the chapel are clear. The gray stone of its high walls was set off by rose-dark wooden pews, their backs and seats polished and smooth. The air was cool, and an ethereal silence descended from the high vaulted ceilings. I remember most vividly the resonance lent by that space to human voice in song, the many hymns sung by a full congregation. There were the soothing ones: "Softly and tenderly Jesus is calling . . . calling all sinners, 'Come home.'" And the spirited ones: "Praise ye the Lord, the Almighty, the King of Creation!" And once, a tenor solo, rich and full: "O brother man fold to thy heart thy brother; where pity dwells the peace of God is there." Even my faltering young voice, attempting to fill up the space, swelled to its own fullness. But the words were not what captured me, even though many of those verses stayed in my quick memory. The melodies drew the music out of me, the ringing notes rising into the sanctuary air, the lyric phrases that traced the edge of beauty for my ear. With the full choir of assembled voices, treble and bass harmonies reverberated up and down my spine, lilting descants offered a tender blessing. Here was comfort instead of guilt and fear. Here I understood reverence. Here I could imagine the holy.

Those weekly Sunday services provided a spiritual measure of our school year, while the academic calendar scheduled our scholastic achievements. Classes from January to October gave us a long vacation to go home over Christmas and a shorter three-week break in May. Our parents would come up to Kodai for a cool interlude during India's hot summer months, and we moved out of boarding to stay with them at Winsford, a compound of residences for the use of Presbyterian families. Winsford was across Kodai Lake from the school, and sometimes we would walk back and forth by way of the looping three-mile perimeter road. The shorter way was across the lake in the broad-beamed lapstrake rowboats of the Kodai Boat Club, a fixture that, like the lake itself, had been built during the earlier British occupation. As boat club members, our family was allowed to use those boats, and my father helped me learn to row them when I was too small to hold both oars. In the mornings we would start down to the lake in plenty of time to get to school. From a small boathouse at the water's edge we would call across to the boat club, "Boatman! Boat please!" Our voices sailed through the air and came back to us from the opposite shore as though they had been heard throughout the giant chapel of sky. In a few minutes, another sound came to us by way of the clouds—the dipping of the oars as the boatman set out from the far shore. As he came closer, we could make out his thin dark figure in the forward boat, the towline pulling a second boat behind. He delivered it with a shy smile and a bowed head, the deference typical of locals toward foreigners. We would give him our thanks in exchange, climb in and start out across the lake ourselves, my father and I, or my brother and I at the oars. I've often thought that had I been old enough to take one of those boats out on my own, I would like to have rowed to the middle of the lake and tried to fill that space of sky with song.

The lakeshore hills in Kodai were scattered with eucalyptus trees. The trees' tall rounded forms softened the landscape and their spicy fragrance filled the air. Long slender leaves—rosy or green—and gray cone-shaped nuts littered the ground, especially in the woods at Winsford. A path to the lake wandered down the hill there among the trees. Between their trunks, one could get a broken view of the water. When I think of that walk through the woods, I remember a distinct sense of juxtaposition, the immediacy of the trees and the open distance out over the lake—the fact of the moment and the anticipation of beyond. I used to shuffle my feet through the dry rustle of eucalyptus leaves and send nuts rolling down the hill in front of me. The trees stood on either side, their pungent fragrance moving through me, their canopy airy enough along this path that the ground was strewn with light. As I walked I could sense without thinking the prospect ahead of me—the damp boathouse, dark inside, its one small pier in the center, perhaps a boat tethered there, dark wood planks and a wrought iron seat back, oars resting on the seats, oarlocks ready, the gentle rocking as we stepped in, the watery slap against the hull, the push with a boat hook that moved us out into the light, and then the easy stroke and glide, afloat under the spread of sky.

What I know now that I didn't then is that those woods and waters were as fundamental in shaping my sensibilities as was Miss Burke with her efforts to temper my soul. The lake and trees provided some of the simple sensations that come early enough in life to ground us without our conscious acceptance or acknowledgment, the specific awareness of the world through our physical experience of it. Woodland and water, motion and stillness, proximity and distance, the present and the anticipated, darkness and light. Nobody told me that a holy spirit might exist there, in that context, in that feeling of physical relation in the natural world. The words to the hymns I learned sang not of Creation itself but of Creation's God. The Bible verses I memorized assured my redemption from sin, but not my connection to the life source in nature. The essential ties were to heaven, not the earth. My fearful faith didn't celebrate the tangible natural evidence of God, except perhaps through the music that, without any need for words, strikes me now as one of the highest human expressions of wonder and praise.

Perhaps the context Miss Burke wanted to convey to us was a holy one, but I have come to think that what was paramount was not holiness so much as authority— a context that provided a sense of meaning that came from outside ourselves. The verb *to mean* has Saxon, Frisian, and German derivations according to the Oxford English Dictionary, among them "to signify; to have in mind, hence also, to love." Our search for meaning comes from a yearning to love, to encounter those things beyond ourselves that take hold of our hearts. Anchored there, they come to have authority. We live by the parameters they provide. Perhaps Miss Burke wanted to shelter us from the difficulties she knew that search would pose by nurturing in us a love she believed would be sustaining. Her efforts eventually worked on me. Toward the end of my tenure in her care, against the wiser advice of my father who knew I didn't really understand, I decided to confirm my belief by joining the church. I wonder now if Miss Burke would have acknowledged the weakness I was too young to see, the tenuousness of a love grounded not in life's experience, but in the reasoning of a faith infused with guilt and fear. And I wonder if she recognized the things we needed to care for most: our families, each other, and a place—a place where we felt we belonged.

My family left India when I was thirteen and moved to a small rural town in northwest Washington. In many respects it was the perfect community to carry on Miss Burke's influences, conservative and deeply Christian, with families of faith who congregated Sundays at the score of churches serving a population of three thousand. But even Lynden was more diverse than anything I had known. Even there, not everyone adhered to a Christian faith. And other commonalities of American life broke through my innocence. Foul language rolled easily off the tongues of my peers, words I'm not sure had ever entered my mind. I met friends whose parents were divorced. I was invited to parties where juvenile romance stirred in dark corners of a family rec room and in the embraces of dancers barely swaying to tender lyrics like Paul McCartney's, "I want her everywhere, and if she's beside me I know I need never care. . . ." Smoking cigarettes and drinking beer were real choices at those parties, no longer pressures I imagined and feared. And though Lynden's conservatism provided a buffer of familiar moral standards, I struggled, like most teenagers, to figure out how I fit in.

But the time was the 1960s. Outside the safety net of that rural all-American community, the country was being forced to face political and ideological ferment that challenged the status quo. The mood in the air struck a certain personal chord. Growing up in another country had given me a different sense of the world from that of my small-town peers. Going away to school had nurtured the independence I so naively embraced when I was seven. By my third year in high school I had proved my father's doubts about my commitment to the church. I stopped going. My fragile faith didn't hold. My parents' faith was strong, but they still understood the adolescent need to explore the parameters of one's own beliefs. Lynden began to seem conventional and small. My two sisters were bringing home the influences of college, the Vietnam War was at its peak, and the music I was listening to sang of a revolution of both heart and mind. My brother managed to avoid the draft, but my father's dedication to Christian service prompted him to volunteer for a month of medical work at a civilian hospital in Vietnam. Listening to his spoken letters recorded againt the constant whutter of military helicopters, I couldn't help but imagine him in danger, but my mother relied on her faith in God's protection. My father's defiance in going, my mother's defiance in believing were sparks of spirit that rubbed off on me. I enrolled in the first four-year class at Evergreen, a new nontraditional college, and set out on an unconventional adult life.

In that spirit, I quit a couple of temporary jobs several years later and decided to go on a trip to Alaska. I was joining the son of family friends who had also done medical work in India. The two of us hardly knew each other, but our families' connection was a slight reassurance for my parents' concerns about our traveling together. I was twenty-six and determined. Tim was a few years younger, fulfilling a long-planned camping and mountain climbing tour of the north—up through Southeast Alaska by ferry, out to Glacier Bay, then into the state's vast interior in the vintage Volkswagen bus he had packed with an array of equipment, supplies, minimal comforts, and canoe and kayak strapped on top. I added my pack and clothes, settled into the front passenger seat, and busied myself with figuring out the protocols. Routines with tent, camp stove, and food weren't hard to learn, but climbing ropes and ice axes were unfamiliar to my hands. The ability to scale rock faces and snow ridges were skills I was expected to learn because being along for the ride meant that I went along with Tim's plans.

That journey took me to places I could not have imagined beforehand. I had never seen retreating blue caverns of glacial ice. I had not sat face-to-face with a mountain range that rose three miles high out of the sea. I hadn't pictured myself cutting steps across a vertical slope of snow hanging hundreds of feet above a valley floor. Or walking a tenuous snow bridge spanning the sheer ice walls of a deep crevasse. I had never felt my life start to give way to the strength of a rising river. I was shaken again and again by the challenges we mounted against the land. My attempts at courage were attempts to feel significant, and again and again I failed. None of these attempts had anything to do with the place itself.

Those conceited ventures were staged against the abiding backdrop of nature's detail and scope. The turquoise milk of a glacial inlet. The quiet watchfulness of a seal. The yellow burst of cinquefoil on a ledge of rock. The graceful fork in the tail of an arctic tern. The rosy light of a three o'clock dawn tipping sharp mountain crests and spilling a blush down their cold white slopes. We had made our way through the watery mountain country of Southeast Alaska. I confronted the landscape time and again without words. Often my body ached and my heart had been wrenched small, and yet here was a presence I could not face down—powerful, indifferent, complex, staggering, sublime. Its lack of humanness offered a curious comfort, a perspective that let me imagine, for the first time, the boundaries of my life being defined and supported by the earth.

Now it was June. We were driving the wide country between lodges and gas stations along the Alaska Highway. The road stretched off to become a thin line that disappeared over the horizon, our tie to the human world. An immense green rolled away from us—the dense forest of spiky black spruce broken up by the hillock and bog of the tundra. Those verdant reaches gradually rose to foothills, then to the low peaks that courted the high snowy summits of the Wrangell Mountains south of us and the Alaska Range north. The land and sky met in a boundless circle around us. We drove and drove and seemed to go nowhere. The mountains loomed closer, only to extend their ranges far into the distance. Rivers cut sweeping valleys, giving shape to the land for miles around. We would skirt them, cross them, climb away, come back again to their high cutbanks or wide gravel bars in braided streams, then finally see them turn and flow out of sight. On and on and on, this vastness, this country defined by no terms but its own. The human scale I was accustomed to was diminished here. Our tent, our canoe, our Volkswagen were my measure and protection, but their adequacy was an illusion. They disappeared against the reach of the tundra, were hardly visible on the slender thread of the Alaska highway that stretched across the openness and into the beyond. The pockets of human habitation at distant points along the highway—perhaps a group of houses, a gas station, a few other buildings—seemed huddled together in their own defense against the expanse. I found it difficult to establish a sense of proximity; everything close at hand got lost in a scale so grand it defied an appropriate response.

I rode along without words as our crowded VW bus rattled down the road. Tim's favorite rock and roll played on the tape deck and filled the car as we drove, a buffer between us and the immensity of the scene. When we stopped to get out and stretch our legs, turned off the car and the music, our simple silence was not enough to accommodate the stillness that pressed against us so absolutely. The sound of our few sentences, rather than carrying any distance, fell at our feet. Everything was too far away and the enormousness of the space was too close. I was more comfortable climbing back in the bus, turning on the music again, and driving along.

The northern summer sun circled the horizon, stretching our days wide and long. The uneasiness perpetuated by that vast landscape settled itself into the passenger

seat with me. I easily recognized the elements of vulnerability and fear. What came more gradually was an acknowledgment of a larger truth that arose out of the
place itself. Humanity was not important here. This was
simply the fundamental, essential earth—its land, its
waters, its vegetation, its skies, its elemental force and
power, its complexity and grace. Creation itself was de-
manding witness, forcing its own recognition. The up-
welling I felt inside was my timid heart rising to meet it.

I was not prepared for that. I had not anticipated the
surge of emotion. I had not known so completely the
inadequacy of both imagination and reason. I had not
considered the possibility that the earth itself could pull
me toward understanding. I had not expected the sense
of calling, the longing to have the wholeness that en-
compassed such a grand horizon find a place within.
"Longing, we say," writes poet Robert Hass, "because desire is full of endless distances." Our rattletrap Volkswagen
rolled on down the road, and a sweet tenor voice on the
tape deck sang with his guitar, "Falling in and out of
love with you, falling in and out of love." I tried to stretch
myself around the swell of my heart. I tried to imagine
a music to fit the landscape and thought of Beethoven's
Ninth Symphony or Keith Jarrett's *Köln Concert*. But the
melodies that came to me were from the hymns that
had filled the sanctuary in that chapel of gray stone.

"Miss Burke, Miss Burke," I thought, "If you want to
see God, if you want to face the Holy Spirit, come and
look, come and witness this."

Of Landscape and Longing

I stared at the wall of snow. It hung almost vertically
from high rock and fell away to talus slopes hundreds
of feet below. A line of steps cut across it, paralleled by
a row of handholds used for balance. Tim had set the
route and waited for me at an outcrop of crumbling rock
on the other side. Whatever faith he had in my novice
ability was blindly rooted in his own desire—to climb
Mount Merriam, a five thousand-foot peak in Glacier
Bay National Park. Whatever confidence I had was awash
in fear. There was no rope between us, no guarantee the
snow would hold, only the unspoken agreement made
when I joined him on his long-planned Alaska trip. I
would take part in whatever adventure he schemed. My
safety mechanism, an ice axe, was a new tool to me and
felt useless in my trembling hands. The helmet I wore
seemed like little protection if the snow were to give
way, or if I were to fall, not be able to stop myself, and
end up on the scree far below.

It was five A.M. The red-and-purple dawn that woke
us had already faded to broad daylight. We had stopped
for the night atop a smaller peak that was on our way to

Merriam, and I had gone again and again to a point where I could see the route we would take—down and across steep snow slopes to a sharp ridge of broken rock that fell away precipitously on either side, across it to the buttresses and faces that climbed to Merriam's summit. The short bivouac had been fitful for me, tormented by dreams of falling, irritated by the sore throat and sinuses Tim had waited three days to get over before he felt ready for Merriam. His impatience made it clear there was no time for me to be sick. This was our last chance for a Glacier Bay climb.

I stood at the edge of the snow wall, waiting for the swell of courage that could start me out across it. Behind me, four thousand feet down the escarpments of the mountain, the milky turquoise water of Glacier Bay lay still, faintly rippled by a breeze. Its western edge marked the rise of the Fairweather Range, a tumult of rock and ice and snow, stretching eighty miles north to south, thirty-five miles to the Gulf of Alaska. The crowd of peaks rose from sea level to twelve, thirteen, fifteen thousand feet, and cradled the glaciers that came down to saltwater, giving the bay its name. The days Tim had been sick had offered us our first full view of the scene, the jagged horizon cutting into a blazing blue sky. I had sat in the cool sun of the early northern summer, that enormous landscape pressing on my mind. My eyes followed the line of the distant shore, rose through scrubby willows up to thrusts of rock scraped clean by ice just a century ago, then to snow, ridges and cornices and walls of it mounting each other at every angle, cresting again and again, climbing finally to the high peaks of that grand mountain range—Crillon, La Perouse, Salisbury, Fairweather—wild and elegant and serene. We were the only people for miles. I tried occupying myself with the swallows swooping down the face of the cliff or the ducks and seals in the spangled water below. Beside me, butterflies fluttered over new summer flowers and up the bay, gigantic icebergs edged their way toward us on the tide. I heard the distant honking high overhead of flocks of Canada geese migrating north, but none of these things could hold my attention. My thoughts returned insistently to those mountains. They were two and three times the size of Merriam and not anything we intended to climb, but they provided imaginary practice: over and over I picked out possible routes and made the assaults, inventing myself as a climber, trying to talk myself into the venture I was obligated to in a few days. The fantasies were fueled both by mistaken notions of the love I thought was at stake and by a fear that haunted me. I wasn't free to let that exquisite place simply be what it was. It had become an adversary, a test of my confidence and strength, of my courage and sensibilities, of my appeal to Tim.

He was waiting. I fought to steady myself as I scanned the slope again. The dread I had tried to hold down pounded in my chest. I cursed my cowardice and Tim's expectations, cursed the snow slope itself. Then something put my feet in motion. They began to find the steps Tim had made. Using the icy handholds for balance, I crept out onto the slope. I tried not to think about where I was, concentrating instead on just going forward, but every movement trembled. My feet quivered into each step while I fought the panic and the tears, knowing I couldn't founder in the middle of the crossing. A will I seemed to have no control over worked to close the gaping distance of snow between Tim and me, but by the time I reached him, I could not stop shaking.

An ascent of Mount Merriam was out of the question. I would not be a safe partner for the rest of the climb.

Our decision to turn back should have been a comfort but wasn't. Tim's disappointment made me ashamed of my fear. The silence it left between us loomed like the snow slope I had just crossed and deepened my humiliation. I hated the sense of feminine inadequacy that trapped me, but could not find the self that knew composure and dignity. The ache in my head and throat had begun to spread to the rest of my body. Everything had slipped out of kilter. The confusion of emotion blurred the terror of going back across that slope, but I was utterly shaken for the rest of the hike back to camp. My feet gave way beneath me. I slid uncontrollably down snow gullies, stumbled and fell in scree. Tim waited without watching, without advice or encouragement. We argued silently about the failure until we reached camp and had other things to tend to. We would leave Glacier Bay in a couple of days.

The work of packing up camp brought some of the relief I needed to untangle the turmoil. I was grateful for the simple task of putting things away. But our taking leave of that place was laced with a swell of sadness. We had spent almost three weeks in Glacier Bay and had explored several islands, coves, and inlets in different parts of the park. We had camped close to those moving rivers of ice on land just recently exposed, land just beginning to seed itself with mountain avens that prepared the soil for the succession in years to come—willow, alder, spruce, hemlock. We had paddled our canoe among icebergs many times our size, walked beside them on beaches where they were stranded by the tide. We had seen seals with their pups, orcas and humpback whales, eagles in the nest, rookeries of puffins and murres. We had weathered days of the rain that nourished that place and finally witnessed the staggering grandeur of the scene. Our attempt at Merriam was to be the culmination of our visit. Now the threat it had posed gave it the weight and pain of an injury that felt like it would never heal.

And yet the anguish floated on a montage of days filled with the magnificence of the place itself. This pocket of wilderness was a time capsule of geological history, a remarkable juxtaposition of ecosystems edging the unusually rapid retreat of ice. There was a newness about the country that made my brief familiarity with it feel like a privilege. I knew the distinct shapes of the Fairweathers' high peaks, the landmarks that figured the shore. I had come to expect the afternoon breeze. I had watched the faces of glaciers change, listened to them break silence with thunder as they dropped towers of ice into the water. I had learned the slender form of the arctic tern, watched cinquefoil and paintbrush bloom. Never before had I been face to face with a landscape that spoke with such delicacy and power of the inherent beauty of the earth. Never had the land been so intimidating as to blind me with the terror of my fears. I could only pray for the vision to return.

We loaded our canoe and paddled across Glacier Bay's west arm to Blue Mouse Cove, where we awaited the tour boat that would pick us up. When it arrived, we learned that we would be spending one more night in the bay in order to accommodate the travel plans of a group of German tourists on board. The captain motored the boat around into Muir Inlet, the other main arm of the bay, and anchored off McBride Glacier for the night. He had agreed to let us put our sleeping bags down on the deck. After dinner, Tim went ashore with some of the crew to explore the area around the glacier. I relished the chance to be alone. My head throbbed with the ache of swollen sinuses that made it difficult to breathe. I climbed into my sleeping bag and listened to the water lapping against the hull of the boat and against icebergs floating nearby. Gradually I realized I was also listening to a familiar melody. In the cabin below me, the Germans were singing Brahms's lullaby in their native tongue. The soft harmonies drifted easily on the night air. I wrapped myself in that comfort and held it close until I slept.

Like clarities that come to us only in our dreams, there are forces that work on the psyche unbeknownst to the conscious mind. That Alaskan landscape had set something in motion in my life. It awakened a sensibility I did not fully understand but could not ignore. Ten months after Glacier Bay, I stood on the forward deck of the ferry *Malaspina* as it steamed through Peril Strait toward Sitka, a hundred miles to the south. The day was a sparkling blue, the sky and water brilliant with spring light that glazed high snows above the forests draping the steep shore. I remembered the Fairweathers, their keen white silhouette against a clear summer sky, and recognized a feeling that seemed to hang in the air: the land was alive. It was itself, not redefined by human design. It imposed itself, came to meet the ferry at every turn rather than waiting for us to arrive. I looked across the distance of water to ridges climbing to summit after summit and winced as my imagination still put me to the test of scaling those peaks one at a time. But I was alone on this journey. My obligations were to myself. Upstairs in the solarium lounge was my backpack with enough belongings to last until I knew if I was going to stay.

Sitka was settled on a shelf wedged into the half crown of mountains that braced it against the cold reach of the North Pacific Ocean. The town is the only major pocket of civilization on an island otherwise rugged and wild: a hundred miles north to south, thirty miles across at its widest point, crest upon crest rising out of the ocean to tower over valleys and lakes, snows and glaciers and forest. Ancient stands of rain-drenched spruce, hemlock, and cedar edge bays and inlets carved into the land. The island and surrounding waters are inhabited by eagle and brown bear, by raven and deer and chickadee, by squirrel and mink and otter. This is a summer place for salmon and thrushes and warblers and hummingbirds. It is a winter place for humpback whales and herring and loons and scoters. Orca, Canada goose, harbor seal, and sea lion know the place too. And humans have known it for centuries. Archaeological evidence puts human populations in Southeast Alaska at least 9,500 years ago. A basket found recently on south Baranof Island confirms that people were gathering food in this area around 3200 B.C. Archaeologists don't assign the basket to a particular culture, but the Tlingit, the indigenous people living here when eighteenth-century European explorers came up the coast, claim the basket as part of their history. Their oral tradition does not give exact dates for their arrival in these parts, but their stories put them here "from time immemorial." Tlingit villages and fish camps spread up and down the Alexander Archipelago and as far north as Yakutat. There are also inland communities in southwest Yukon Territory and northwest British Columbia. The Tlingit that settled on this island called it *Shee. Sitka* is an Anglicized version of their name for a place on the island's outer, or seaward, edge.

The peopled niche of the town provided a safe harbor for me, a community to participate in, but the place itself pervaded everything, breathing with a strength that marked the limitations of humanity, an unruly collaboration of fitful ocean and ragged land. I eased my way in, trusting what was socially familiar first, and warily courting the country. I learned stories, place names, trails, and trees, watched tides and storms, surrounding myself with information as though knowledge was protection against the landscape that beckoned so strongly, but still gave shape to my fear. The calling was elemental, my heart answering directly to the earth. And the fear went straight to my bones, nourished by the lingering torment that would not let me forget the enormous power inherent in the land and its absolute indifference toward me. The paradox was steady company, an ongoing rivalry between desire and apprehension, instinct and will. While I gradually became acquainted with the place, my spirit rallied and faltered in its presence.

The late northern light of summer took me out on the porch one evening in June. As I walked outside, I was greeted by a single musical note, soft and keen and clear as glass, that held itself for a moment, then overflowed to a melody cascading into the evening air. I stopped in the silence left behind. The song came again, the pitch slightly higher, the first note, simple and pure, breaking into the fluted lyric that rolled across the twilight. I stood where I was, scanning the trees to find the singer. Again the song, this time my ear catching the slight trill that edged the last notes before they faded into stillness. I was captive. Again and again and again the song, pouring clarity and ease into the summer night. The longer I listened, the more it seemed like an offering, given for the sake of itself. I let it pull me farther and farther into the evening as it filled the air time after time, the consistency of voice a reassurance, the variation of pitch each time a gentle surprise.

The singer sang on tirelessly and only stopped when the light gave way to dusk. I savored the echoes of the last notes as they floated off into that darkening breath, then turned themselves into silence. Nothing moved. A tranquility had descended that dispelled all need. I wanted nothing more than the cool air on my face. The quiet I felt within was something I had not known for a long time.

I quickly learned that that communion of song had been offered by the male hermit thrush, a remarkably plain brown bird of spring and summer in the hillside forests of Southeast Alaska. He sang to lure the female thrush into his territory and to ward off other male thrushes who might trespass. For me, his song contained the solace of a concord that existed outside of what was human, a purity of sound uncluttered by thought, a weightlessness without the press of matter, a clarity free from the siege of the questioning mind. His cadences were instinctual, not imposed, his repeated harmonies fresh every time. He had enticed me out of the tangle of self-consciousness into the intimacy of the world just beyond my door—cedar and hemlock and huckleberry all bathed in light and song.

The hermit thrush sang on through midsummer, calling me out on my porch evenings, his song drifting through an open window into early morning sleep. His serenades put the day to rest and sang light into the dawn. His singing urged me to take the time to pay attention. It marked the season, a cycle of renewal and possibility. Those simple lyrical notes were diffusing boundaries I had lived with much of my life and replacing them with a sense of narrative, of relationship. Those strands of music delineated the intricacies of species, habitat, purpose, time of day, season. Each time the song hit my ear, it worked to shift my awareness and allowed me to reshape my sense of self, let me hear the thrush's voice in my voice, think of the breath of huckleberry in my breath, feel the tenacity of cedar in my bones, sense the pulse of all life reflected in my own. There was no need to prove my humanness. If I was open and willing, the relationships inherent in the world outside my door could proportion my life, help me understand where I belonged.

The thrush's song was the gentlest of catalysts that helped me acknowledge I was seeking an essential faith. I wanted a balance for the patterns instilled in me by social design. I wanted the meter of that greater rhythm to define what was possible and show me my limitations. I wanted tolerance to ground my desire, respect to ground my fear. I wanted to be able to find again and again that quiet within.

And yet I found that faith came not as readily to a willful mind as to a receptive heart. Faith was nurtured by unexpected moments—when a certain slant of light showed me a familiar grove of trees as I'd never seen them before, shining in their own sacredness. When the violent wind and rain of a winter storm broke to the command of a resplendent sun, evoking authorities far greater than any I could know. When the line and space of an unfamiliar landscape touched and comforted me like someone who loved and knew me well. Those moments were points of witness. They stopped me the same way the hermit thrush's song had, exposed me directly to the vitality that gives way to life. They took their place beside my fear and let me feel the healing power of that which is beautiful.

On a fall day a few years later, while visiting a friend in Haines, a town north of Sitka by a hundred fifty miles, I pedaled a bicycle up the Haines highway along the Chilkat River. Across the wide bed of the river rose the Chilkat Range, high snowy peaks which joined the Takhinsha Mountains to form the northwest corner of Glacier Bay National Park. This was the closest I had been since the Mount Merriam climb. That ache lay just over the mountains, on their southeast side. The Chilkat's broad valley was unlike anything found in Glacier Bay. The sweep of space lured me off the bicycle and out onto the sandbars that edged the channels of the river. In the wet sand were the tracks of those who had come before me—wolf and moose. I made my way with them toward a bank that held some of the Chilkat's swift water. Along it were bear tracks, sow and cub, heading north, following salmon upriver. The wolf and moose tracks joined them. I lined my footprints up alongside theirs, cautiously scanning that wide openness for moving forms. Out in the middle, a low fog drifted up the valley from the river's mouth. As it moved toward me the fog became luminescent, lit by a fiery autumn sun. These shining mists wafted past me, following bear, moose, wolf, and salmon, as though returning to some source, the spirit of the river going home. My tracks were the trail of one who was learning to see.

Consecration by Water

The kind arms of Reverend Vasantrao Rambhise held me
as he stood in front of the Vengurla church congregation.
My infant head rested in his palm and my tiny hands
waved about in the holy air. So my parents told me. They
stood with him beside the baptismal font while my sisters' and brother's young white faces watched from the
first pew. Behind the altar, a tall scrollwork cross set in the
wall let in lacy streams of morning light. I wore a little
white dress, the color of purity, of moist air gathered into
cloud, of ocean spray and foam. The water of the sacrament waited in a small basin. Vasantrao spoke in Marathi
to my parents and to the congregation, smiling about this
new life. He smiled as he looked down at me. Then, recit-
ing the Marathi words of the baptismal liturgy, he splashed
my small head once, twice, three times in honor of the
Holy Trinity, consecrating this life, offering it sacred
blessing.

A monsoon downpour approached across the distance, ushered over the landscape by fragrantly damp air. The drumming was a faint murmur at first, then a wider hissing rustle, then a crowded clatter peppering the tiles of our roof. The red dirt of the driveway became pocked with raindrops. Leaves on the garden bushes began to glisten. Water started to fall from the eaves, first a drip and a drip, then a trickle, then a steady narrow stream. Coolness moved in through the screened windows of the house. The shower relieved the air's tired heat. Its rhythm attuned the ear, wakened the mind's impulse to look out. This rain delicious. This rain long awaited. This rain a renewal. This rain earth's sacrament, consecrating all living things.

II.

Mr. Reble, the chaplain at Kodai School in southern India, stood hip deep in the pool in front of the easy cascade of Fairy Falls. His white pastoral robes floated and billowed about his legs. His arms were spread slightly, welcoming the occasion and its initiate. Memorized lines of scripture rolled through his voice and then the ceremony's introductory sacred words. Then he joined me and the other witnesses on shore in the baptismal hymn:

> Just as I am without one plea
> But that Thy blood was shed for me
> And that Thou bidst me come to Thee
> O Lamb of God, I come, I come.

My young voice mixed hesitantly with the older so-
pranos and altos and tenors, moving naively from verse
to verse, while Ellen Reeder, wearing a full-skirted white
dress with a fitted sleeveless bodice, waded into the water.
The spotless yards of fabric swirled about her legs as she
made her way across the pool to Mr. Reble. If the water
was cold, neither of them acknowledged it.

I stood on the shore among the onlookers, intimidated
and fascinated, my eyes alternately downcast and wide.
The graveness of the occasion made me nervous. The easy
flowing melodies and lyrics of the hymn saturated me
with as much holiness as I could muster. I don't remember who else was in the audience, how the witnesses
were invited or selected to come, for it wasn't the full
school congregation. And I don't remember how we got
to Fairy Falls, a mile or two from the school campus. But
now Ellen was at Mr. Reble's side in the pool and the hymn
was coming to a close. We all stood together for a brief
moment without words, the water a continuum, spilling
easily down the wall of rock, splashing into the pool, rippling around the baptist and his initiate, moving out to
the pool's edges, lapping at our feet.

And then the words of the baptism sacrament, exchanged over the sound of that water, and the moment
of consecration. My heart rose into my throat. Mr. Reble
put his arm behind Ellen's waist and lowered her backward into the pool to anoint her head, first *in the name of
the Father,* then *in the name of the Son,* then *in the name
of the Holy Spirit.*

Ellen stood again on her own, dripping, chilled,

cleansed. My heart found its way back to where it belonged, but it was pounding. I wondered if she felt protected, if she noticed a palpable shift in her being, if her life felt as if it had taken a turn, if she saw it stretched out now in front of her like a clear and shining path, if she felt lighter and more at ease or weighted with responsibility, having been consecrated as one of God's chosen in front of all those witnesses.

There must have been towels and dry clothes, perhaps a ride back to the Kodai School campus, but those details escaped my memory. Perhaps Ellen and Mr. Reble went together, finishing off the occasion with some final words of concern and counsel. Or maybe Ellen's friends welcomed her, congratulated her, asked her the questions that piqued my imagination. How did she feel? Was it cold? Had she been nervous? Was she glad it was over? And when she lay alone in her bed that night, perhaps she welcomed the privacy of the darkness, the chance to be alone with her affirmed faith, her new blessedness. Perhaps the voice of God was there on the other side of her prayers, reassuring her, easing her into sleep.

Below the dam that had been built to create Kodai Lake, water poured down a gently stepped streambed of broad rounded stones, collecting in little pools, then spilling over to the next rock below, spreading itself over that surface of stone like a moving glass curtain until it fell over another edge to another pool where it splashed and swirled around itself and around my hands and ankles that delighted in its coolness, its wetness, its ease. Down in the dimness of the pool, tiny black tadpoles squiggled about, their squirming tails scooting them around my feet, eluding my fingers. A slippery green layer of life edged the rocks. I made my way from pool to pool, squatting down to peer into the water's little deeps, secret pockets in the cool wet darkness. The stream burbled past me. Leaves floated like miniature boats swirling in small eddies, getting caught together in nooks where the water let them rest, then washed them out and over a lip of stone to the next little catchbasin and the next, the water flowing down and down and down, following the contours of the hillside, finding its way to other freshets and rivulets, joining them, gathering momentum, cutting deeper and wider, tumbling over itself, under shaded canopies, out in the tropical sun, washing tree root and soil and stone, splashing plant and flower, cooling and moistening the air, falling down and down the face of the mountain, down and down to the flat and open country of India's hot plateau, into a slow and muddy river rolling heavily across the stretch of dry and reaching land to the edge that meets ocean and ocean and ocean, the planet's blessing this water that wraps our blue jewel of life, our home, spinning in the vast and holy darkness.

III.

The McKinley River bar was almost a mile across. Milky glacial water swept along the river's channels, some of them little more than ankle deep, others over my hips.

Tim and I were hiking out after several days in the Denali Park backcountry. The peaks of the Alaska Range lay twenty or thirty miles behind us, marching across the high horizon. Tim was leading the way across the river bar. He tested the channels of the McKinley as we came to them, one and another and another. We both carried heavy packs. I followed his routes across each stream, unable to see the boulders and rocks that held the bottom or got tumbled along by the swift moving water. Channel by channel we made our way across that mile, no trees, no animals, no other people to watch or guard or guide us. I used a walking stick to steady myself as my feet and legs became numbed by the glacial water—solid footing there, then there, then there, each step tenuous at first then certain, tenuous then certain, measured anxiousness holding me against the water's strong current. I was top-heavy with the forty-five pounds on my back and had to concentrate to maintain my balance.

We had driven along these wide Alaskan river bars on our way to Denali. They cut their wide swaths through the landscape, centuries of water moving rocks and gravel and sand. They enticed and impressed us. We had been lucky enough to lose our canoe and not our lives to the springmelt swollen Matanuska when, on the briefest of river runs, a terrified impulse stood me up in the bow and prompted me to throw one leg over the gunwale to find the solid bank that held that river's deep cold rush of water.

The McKinley's braided channels made it wider and shallower, but it was equally cold. I was feeling my way with leaden feet, my heavy hiking boots even heavier and saturated with the icy chill. The banks of the channel were too far ahead and behind to offer assurance. I was treading the eternity of those bitter cold moments, willing my way to the far cutbank through the momentum and weight and strength of water.

And then I was down. My pack was on top of me, pushing my face into the stream. I fought to roll over, banging my knees and elbows and shins on the boulders hidden in the murky moving cold. Finally I managed to find the sky, but I couldn't get my feet back under me. I thrashed about uselessly, floating uncontrollably downstream. The force of water carried me along a sacred edge where life meets its source and its beginnings. I remember seeing Tim running along the bank, too far away to be of help. I remember struggling and struggling and then a moment when, exhausted beyond my means, I felt as if I could just slip into sleep. I was tempted to give way to that moment when my body stopped moving and I felt the solid ground of a sandbar beneath me. The earth held me firm. I was on my back with my pack still under me holding me down, but I strained to sit up, lifting that waterlogged weight with every single muscle in my body. At last I was still. I could see the world again. My arms found their way out of the straps of the pack and it fell beside me. I sat on that holy piece of ground and wept.

That night, in the safety of my sleeping bag, my exhaustion lulled me into a sleep that drifted uneasily along the earthly side of the McKinley's swift cold. I woke in the dusky northern midnight with a broken-bone pain in one wrist. There was no clear explanation, only the certainty of feeling. I made myself as comfortable as I could and let the pain be whatever it was. There, in the wide and open darkness, that ache was enough—enough to affirm a life that the earth had shaken and humbled and blessed.

Soundings

Whales again, at sunrise on a frigid November morning. Humpback. A lone one this time. Its steamy shot of air bursts from the water into apricot light. The dark back with pointed dorsal fin breaks the surface, curves slightly into colored air, then sinks into water. The world that holds this morning has been caught by winter. High snowy ridges across the bay whet their edges on the cold. Below, frosted hemlock and huckleberry trim the forest and patchy ice rises on the tide. I stand at the window, uneasily anticipating the bitter chill outside. It seems to have slowed everything within its reach, sent blood and sap deep, leaving stillness and silence. But there is a second spout. The whale's hot breath, spangled with light, lingers in the cold air as its back rises again and disappears. In another few seconds a third spout. Through binoculars I can see the whale's blowhole, follow the line of its back as it rises once more, arching higher this time, the peak of its dorsal fin crowning the arc that continues until the thick wedge of tail raises the whale's flukes to finish the curve. They slip gracefully below the surface in the dive that takes the whale deep. In these few minutes of the whale's surfacing, the icy fist of the morning has lost its grip. Here is a massive blood-hot life, holding its own, steaming into the cold, a welcome demonstration of the pervasive balance, the tension that holds the world. Warmed by this reminder, I am braced against the sharp edge of winter.

Humpback whales frequent this area enough that they often move through my days. When I came here more than a decade ago, I didn't realize I would be living in a sphere that overlapped so consistently with theirs. Whales had existed in a remote realm of mystery I assumed would always withhold its clues from me. Now I find the rhythms of their surfacing familiar, the series of blows before the deep dive, the easy rise and fall of the back, the arc that brings the show of flukes. Becoming accustomed to the whales' presence has been paradoxical for it has meant getting used to the extraordinary. In time, I've found this paradox turning on itself and becoming another: the marvel of these animals has not diminished with familiarity. In fact, what I know of the whales is merely an outline of their movements, but the points where that line intersects my world are points where delight gives way to reverence, points that resonate with wonder. The whales' presence stays with me long after they've gone. The extended line of their black bodies breaks air with specific form. The light glinting off their backs brands itself in my eye. Their flukes have imprinted a shadow on my mind, and their explosive breaths echo in my ear. The sheer mass of body and the strength with which they move are difficult to comprehend since they surface intermittently from a world not readily available to my eyes. But witnessing the breach of a whale, seeing it propel itself all the way out of the water and fly into the air, watching the upheaval as its forty tons hit water again, I am struck silent by a kind of power that will never be mine to understand. The wake of that whale's splash washes my memory still.

Rumors that humpbacks were in the area prompted some friends and me to arrange a chartered whale-watching trip my first winter in Alaska. There was no guarantee we would see whales, but we couldn't pass up a chance none of us had known. In our minds, these were spiritual creatures that transcended the natural world. They held the essence of something we didn't know how to name but wanted to believe in. They were the key, perhaps, to one of life's great secrets. Encountering them was a dream almost too magnificent to come true.

The day of our trip brought cold wind and rain. The cabin of the boat was littered with boots, sweaters, rain gear, cameras, and binoculars. We headed north to the bay where whales had been sighted and, almost as soon as we entered the bay, began to see spouts: first two, then another pair and another. We greeted them with whoops of excitement, amazed that our dreams were materializing before our eyes. Our skipper was the only calm one among us. An experienced whale watcher, he was keenly aware of their sensitivity to intrusion and approached them cautiously, running the boat's engine at a slow idle, trying to let them know we were there but meant no harm. The whales seemed to pay little attention and allowed us to get close enough to see that they were feeding. Their surfacing was accompanied by a flurry of birds—eagles, gulls, murres, goldeneyes, grebes—all attracted by whatever feed was in the area. As if this were not enough, there were sea lions and otters close by. This testimony to the abundance of life in these waters intoxicated us. We sang to the whales, hugged each other, laughed at our giddiness, and eventually chattered ourselves to silence as we watched show after show of spouts and backs, flippers and flukes.

Looking back, I recall significant pauses that punctuated the whirl of exhilaration that day, interruptions caused by a simple but profound realization. The whales were not what we had thought. They certainly were magnificent but not transcendent. They moved in the same water we did, edged the same shoreline and rocks. Their breaths, warm like ours, steamed into the same cold air. Our proximity to them forced us to recognize not some spiritual essence unique to them, but rather the systematic grace of intricate relationships that are the very foundation of our mutual existence, of the natural world. It is this grace that we, as human beings, can choose or not to acknowledge, giving it the reverence it is due. Sometimes, however, it is not a matter of choice. Sometimes we simply see, then swallow our inadequate words and hold that moment in our hearts.

Seven o'clock on a summer morning. The sun has been up for hours, and my eyes have to adjust to full daylight as I reach over to turn off the alarm. No sooner does the ringing stop than I hear the explosion. My mind flips through the possibilities, and in seconds I've recognized the sound. Whales. I am instantly wide awake at the window, watching three dark hulks sinking below the water's surface. They are closer to shore than I have ever seen them, just beyond some rocks that are fifty yards from the beach. The whales have been feeding in the bay for the past few days. From the way they surfaced—all three at once—and from the show of heads rather than backs or flukes, I assume they are indulging again. The moment my eyes lose them to the water, I find bathrobe and slippers and my way downstairs to the porch outside.

The water is a sheet of glass, mirroring the light of the morning. The air is cool. If there are sounds, I don't hear them. My attention is fixed on that spot just beyond the rocks. The conditions are perfect for watching what I know is to come. I stand silent, arms crossed for a bit of warmth, determined to be a witness. I don't have to wait more than a few minutes before the bubbles begin to ripple the surface. They start at a fixed point and move clockwise in an arc first away from shore, then back toward me in a continuing line around to the point where they began. The circle completes itself and in seconds the water explodes in what appears to be mass confusion: the gaping mouths, warty heads, thrashing flippers and spouting blowholes of three forty-foot whales. A rush of noise echoes through the bay. Here on the porch there are only the silent exclamations my heart pounds to my brain.

What I am witnessing is not confusion at all but the final movement in an intricate dance humpback whales sometimes engage in when they feed. The technique is called bubble net feeding. Diagrams I have seen of it show a whale diving down to get underneath a school of krill or small fish, then blowing bubbles as it swims gradually upward in a spiral. The rising bubbles eventually form a cylindrical net around the krill or fish, effectively herding them into a confined area. The whale then lunges to the surface inside the circumference of the cylinder, mouth open, engulfing everything in its way. These are not toothed whales; instead, they have long tapered plates of baleen hanging from their top jaws, arranged like teeth on a comb. The baleen is pliable when wet and frayed along one edge. The hundreds of plates along each side of the mouth act like a sieve, trapping food and letting water pour back out into the ocean. As the whales swallow their latest catch, they loll about at the surface for a few moments, as though relishing the enormous bite. Then comes the series of spouts and arching backs that precede the deep dive that will let them begin the process again.

What is intriguing is how and why whales take part

in the process together. What relationship do they have to each other? Is this group feeding activity a cooperative effort? If so, do the whales delegate roles in the performance? Which whale or whales blow the bubbles? How do they position themselves in order to get the completed motion, the timing just right? The questions surface like so many bubbles of the unknown. I marvel at the elegant form given to such a fundamental act of living, at its precision and efficacy, at the intelligence that conceived it.

As I get accustomed to the company of whales, I realize they are redefining the parameters of my world. Thinking of myself in relationship to them helps me understand proportion, focuses my attention on the connections we each have to the continuum of nature. The whales have shown me what it means to live in an animate world, one in which process and motion are constants, forces that render life. This is not a new sensibility, but a long forgotten one stirred back into being. The movement of whales through my days has reawakened me to the form and detail of living things: not only the distinct line that is humpback, but the specific flowering of huckleberry, the particularity of winter wren song, the quality of air in season. Otherness. That which is outside myself. To know my place in the arrangement is to foster a sense of kinship, to know how to behave. Such knowing requires a willingness to accept human limitation and a deep regard for the exquisite relationships that hold the natural world.

I would that this knowledge were an inherent sense, as necessary as food, as easy as breathing. It comes not so naturally, but feels that essential. It comes more easily if I can leave myself open to wonder.

On a mild June afternoon, I set out in an aluminum canoe to try to catch up with a lone humpback whale. This canoe has been modified for rowing, a small advantage in the effort to keep up with this powerful swimmer. The whale has been bubble net feeding, grazing widely throughout the bay. I pursue it out of a simple desire for closeness, proximity. I want nothing between us but air and water and the bottom of my boat. I want the noise of its sharp breaths fresh in my ears. I want to see the specific blackness of its skin, watch the water pour off its flukes as they rise. I want a true sense of its size. Without binoculars, I want to discern the swell of its blowhole, note the pattern of white markings on the underside of its tail when it dives. I want to make out the ring of bubbles that will mark its presence, hold my breath while I wait for the whale to appear.

The day is calm, the conditions just right for rowing. A steady stroke of the oars moves the canoe swiftly over the water. I head toward the vicinity where the whale last surfaced, having no clue where it might come up again. Nearing some islands half a mile from shore, I pause to adjust the oars. As soon as I stop rowing, my attention is alerted to a resonant tone permeating the whole area around me. The sound is like the ringing of crystal, a pure single note vibrating in my ears. I glance about quickly, trying to discern where it is coming from. Turning to look behind me, I notice the curving line of bubbles marking the water's surface several hundred feet away. As the bubbles move around in their circle, the ringing continues. I barely have time to make a connection between the two when the circle of bubbles is completed and the ringing stops. I am stunned. Not only do these whales feed with a flourish of form, but they add music to this performance! I am so taken by the idea that the whale's lunge to the surface startles me. I can only stare as it lounges about, swallowing its mouthful of food. The questions begin to flood my mind while the whale rights itself, blows a few sharp breaths, and sounds with a show of flukes.

Once I am free to move again, I ease back into the steadiness of rowing and head in the same direction the whale seemed to be going when it went down. With each stroke of the oars, my imagination pulls at the truth about the whale's song. Why and how? Why didn't I hear it from the porch that morning? I can't help the questions, and having no answers only fuels my urge to encounter the whale as completely and directly as I can. I want its presence lodged firmly in my mind. I want a constant reminder that this whale is an integral part of the world. I want to keep myself open to wonder.

I have rowed some distance now and have seen no sign of the whale. Any assumption of where it might surface would simply be a guess, so I decide to stop rowing, drift and wait for the next rising. I am in the middle of a wide channel, a mile or more from either shore. The canoe seems especially small in the expanse of water, but there is no wind and swells from the ocean beyond are small and gradual. The freedom of wide open air is welcome, and I feel safe. I scan the distance of this watery stretch for signs of the whale. There are none. The only apparent motion is that of a few gulls riding the air. I notice some larger boats a long way off and think perhaps the whale is theirs to watch now, that it has moved on. But then the ringing begins. It seems to be coming directly up through the bottom of the canoe. My eyes dart around the immediate area and find the bubble ring forming on the starboard side, only thirty feet away. In the few seconds I have, my mind races through the possibilities. I can quickly get out of the way or I can stay put. I am fairly confident the whale won't come up underneath me, but its lunge to the surface could generate waves that would catch the canoe sideways. I have a life vest on, but there is no flotation in the canoe and no boat close by to pluck me out of the water should I go in. I know how cold the water is, but I may never have a chance to be this close to a whale again.

I stay where I am. The whale's song fills me. My heart pounds out its own accompaniment, and I am not afraid. I watch the circle of bubbles define itself. In its center, the water boils with fish, their silver backs flashing in the light. They are driven into a frenzy by their captivity, trying without a chance to escape. The bubbles complete the circle, the ringing stops, and in a matter of moments I am looking directly into the enormous mouth of the whale, pink and fleshy and spotted with gray. The dark tunnel of its throat extends into the water. Its accordion jaw balloons out to hold everything it took in on its way up, and water begins to pour from its baleen plates. The slap of a warty flipper keeps it at the surface where it rolls about lazily. If the whale is aware of my presence, it is unconcerned and matter-of-factly goes about its routine. I watch it blow and surface twice, see and hear the air burst from its blowhole, run my eyes over its back gleaming in summer light. It blows a third time, arches its body sharply and raises its flukes in the grand motion of the deep dive. White underneath, bordered in black, they slide silently into the water.

I sit motionless a moment, then reach forward with the oars and realize my whole body is trembling. The day has been filled. I steady myself with each stroke and head home.

Winter once again, and the whales are back. Each time they appear, I am struck by the mark they leave on my days—the awareness of an order that elicits my regard, the swell of a reverent delight. I return home late one night after an evening with friends. Before going into the house, I walk to the edge of the porch for a few minutes with the darkness. The sky is black and speckled with stars, the air still and cold. Out of the silence, the sound: whales blowing. I linger, wishing I could stay the hours but leave them to the night, imagining their black forms in the darkness, the sleek wet backs lit by the stars.

The Pleasure It Can Be
to Walk on the Earth:
A Meditation

In memory of Jack and Margaret Calvin

The roots along this trail map out the pace of my step. Up and over this one, around another, down, step, down, step, step, down. This one I use as a foothold, that one marks the edge of the trail. A raveled web, they spread over the hillside, holding it in place. The soils that cover them are spongy and cushion my walk. I step down again, carefully placing my feet between the gnarls curling out of the ground, right foot first, then left, down high steps, my footfall heavy, jarring the ground and shaking rainwater from the trees above. On down to a small footbridge across a stream. I no longer need to watch my step and can let my eyes rise to the sweep of a slight hemlock arching over the trail where it begins to climb at an easy slope and skirt the side of the hill. My stride evens out. Ahead of me, through breaks in the trees, I can see the shimmer of Thimbleberry

Bay and Eastern Channel, the waterways that place me in the context of Baranof Island, Southeast Alaska, the North Pacific Ocean. I move toward the light, past the striped pyramidal rock at the base of one tree, past the squirrel hole at the base of another. When the trail begins to drop again, I can see the roof of the house. Down, step, down, step, step, down to the cut rounds laid in the slope as stairs—three and then eleven, my fingers running along the rope handrail, down, down, and down, then off on to my porch.

Each day, leaving and coming home, I walk this quarter-mile meander between my house and garage through a forest, a congregation of yellow cedars that chose this slope to share with western hemlock and a scattering of Sitka spruce. The trail skirts their trunks, uses their roots, follows the contours on which they grow. The trees rise on either side of it to eighty, ninety, one hundred feet or more, their boughs interlocking to form a high canopy that defines the light below. To move through them is to move through centuries climbing toward the sky. To consider their years is to consider steadfastness and endurance. I acknowledge them as I go—this one twisted, that one true, these two leaning against each other, creaking in the wind. They stand without thought or word, but with presence. My walks among them are repeating wooded intervals, a form of ritual in my days. The trail through them leads me out into the world and guides me home. The ritual of going is one of preparation, the ritual of returning one of release. The trees complement these rituals with constancy and duration. They are reminders of things that hold.

This forest is not a prime one. Its trees are second growth, slender, their similar diameters telling the story of a competitive scramble for light. Among them are a few larger ones of an older generation that stood by as younger trees gained their ground. They are all rooted in ten-thousand-year-old volcanic ash covering an east-facing slope. The poorly drained soil enticed the cedar and hemlock more than the spruce. History and circumstance have created a fair share of irregularities. Looking up, I notice the witches'-broom scattered widely among the hemlocks, deformed branch clusters caused by parasitic dwarf-mistletoe. A lot of the cedars first grew horizontally at their bases before curving their trunks upward, as though building in a compensating stronghold against a once sliding hillside. Here and there, the heavy black trunks of Sitka spruce rise straight up, tight rounds scaled evenly with bark or knobbled with stubbed branches and burls. Scattered in the spaces between, stumps of the old forest nourish a variety of lichens. Mosses spread over downed trees and the forest floor, edging the trail in plushness, green—complex miniature worlds at the feet of this towering one. Huckleberry and menziesia find enough light under the canopy, skunk cabbage enough moisture beside the little stream, uncommon orchids the open dampness of a short slope beneath a mass of rock.

If there is a single prominent substance here, it is water. The area's one hundred inches of annual rain saturate the forest, which, in turn, exudes moisture, steaming in bright sun, softening the air with its dampness. As if the rain were not enough, the trees snag fog and mist in their branches, pulling the water-laden fleece to themselves. Out in the open stretches, dew collects on blueberry and dwarf dogwood. Inside the forest, boughs drip incessantly after a storm. The swollen ground is springy underfoot. In a winter cold snap, the freeze pulls the water from the topsoil, leaving tiny dirt pillars rimmed with frost. I marvel at them because I see them so seldom. I am more accustomed to the splash of water under my boots, to the wet brush of huckleberry across my sleeve, to that one cold drop that finds its way down the back of my neck.

These discomforts, if they may be called such, come with the choice to live away from a road. They are ones that Jack Calvin accepted when he bought this nine acres above Thimbleberry Bay in 1953. The trail that led through the forest at that time was constructed of planks laid across parallel logs. It stayed low on the hillside, following a stream, then climbed sharply to take you to the road. The problems of maintaining a wooden trail prompted Calvin to put in an alternate path along a different route that switchbacked up the hill from the original house on the beach. When he and his second wife, Margaret, built a new house above a different stretch of the shore in the mid-1970s, a spur trail was called for. That second house is where I now live; that trail is the one that has fixed itself in my mind. Calvin's feeling for the lay of the land helped define a route that avoided obstacles but also catered to a comfortable gait for the average person. The pacing of the trail describes what Jack Calvin knew—the shape of the land, the pleasure it can be to walk on the earth.

It must have suited Calvin to have that pleasure be an integral part of the place he considered home. A house contains important comforts, but here those expand to a sense of belonging that can provide good company from the road all the way down to the water's edge. That sense comes only with a willingness to accept what is here, to know the place on its own terms, and it has more to do with familiarity than ownership. Years walking over the same ground, knowing it by night and day, in moonlight and shadow, rain and wind, mist and snow, in the brilliance of a clear summer morning. This feeling of belonging welcomes me each time I walk the trail. My feet anticipate the steps, my body expects the turns, my mind roams in the spaces of the forest. I have been taken by this place in ways I do not understand. I am a willing party to its forms and moods in return for sustenance of spirit. The forest offers itself continually. In the midst of my coming and going, it remains.

Near the top of the hill is the only stretch of trail open to the sky, where it crosses a thirty-foot swath cleared for power lines running from a hydroelectric dam into town. The openness shifts habitat, point of view. From the lower edge of the cut, my eyes can follow the continuing rise of this hillside up a steep shoulder to the stone summit of Mount Verstovia looming three thousand feet above. To the east, the massif of Bear Mountain, to the west over far trees, the sky-long reach toward ocean. One gains distance here, but not space. The path narrows in this section, and the ground is crowded with sphagnum moss, dwarf dogwood, five-leaved bramble, fern-leaved golden thread. Early and Alaska blueberry spread above them. Cedar and spruce and hemlock seedlings fight their way back. Still, the trail here moves out of shadow and becomes marked by light, showing itself to the sun, to endless variations of sky. In the late dusk of a June evening, the way is lit by hundreds of white dogwood blossoms, earthly stars strewn over the ground. Blueberries plump themselves and ripen here in summer's long light. On cold clear nights, I stop here to watch the undulating curtains and darting spears of the aurora borealis decorate the darkness. Here, spangled snows reply to winter moons.

Going up the hill, this exposed area foreshadows the world I approach as I head into town. Going down, I pass through the cut early on in my walk and head into the privacy of trees. Admission means maneuvering through the most convoluted roots along the trail. My steps set up a motion—downward, forward, side to side, my foot placement the same almost every time. When the trail levels out, I am free simply to be in the forest. The trees allow me to use the passage as I please. Some days my walk is a restless interior one, self-centered and consumed. Other days are so wet I do nothing but resist the rain. What I enjoy most are days when a switch of mind lets me lose self-consciousness and feel the forest that surrounds me: the juxtaposition of cedar hemlock cedar, each holding its place as I walk in the airy room between them. The vertical space they define. The patterned light in their high boughs. The strength accumulated in each trunk. The silent statement they make about my place in a larger scheme. The forest spreads for miles. I have the girth of a single tree. I move upright but small in a towering world. The forest shelters me and pushes me toward a wisdom that I need.

Though I often walk the trail by myself, I am seldom alone in these woods. A small population of red squirrels shares these acres, and the rattle of their voices breaks into my walk any season. My ear's finer tuning picks out the pips and cheeps of junco and chickadee, who are year round residents too. When the air begins to warm and the light to linger past late afternoon, their voices are joined by those of other birds. Varied thrush and winter wren have stayed the winter and are the early singers that mark the spring, the trilled single note of one, the long chattering melody of the other preparing the air for a chorus to come. Robin and kinglet soon add their parts, but what I eagerly await is the crystalline arpeggio of the hermit thrush rippling the twilight. I smile with pleasure at its clarity. The thrush has made way for summer. The orange-crowned warbler joins in now with its softer trill, the Townsend's with its piping notes. Finally, the Swainson's thrush arrives, its spiraling song climbing the air. When I walk the woods these mornings and evenings, the serenade of birdsong is rich company, lilting melodies strung from tree to tree, shimmering sound filling late and early light, rising to rain or mist or sun. I try not to be a disturbance. I walk carefully. I am filled listening.

I have silent company in the forest too. Any morning

from late spring to early fall I catch the webs of spiders across my face as I walk between the huckleberry and menziesia. I am as tortured by their ticklish strands across my face as they must be by my destruction of their webs each day. The spiders' seasonal companions are the slugs, green with black spots or banana white, their six- to eight-inch-long soft bodies shining with slime, oozing slowly toward another feeding, their sticky trails glistening on the ground. They are regular compatriots for months. Their scarcity is a sign the air has cooled. It is without song again. I listen then for the hammering of a woodpecker or the flicker's whistle and know the days have turned toward their journey into winter. The forest feels like a once teeming house from which many inhabitants have gone. I settle in to its quiet darkness and wait for nights when I can walk among the trees and hear the cold popping in their branches. And then the season's first snowfall—the chilled hush in the woods, the brightened light between the tree trunks, the squeaky crunch of my boots, the bare line of huckleberry and menziesia retraced in icy crystals, the persistent green of low blueberry or moss elaborating the whiteness of the snow.

The Calvin house where I live is at the foot of the trail, tucked into a small clearing among the trees just above Thimbleberry Bay. The house has the feeling of a private room within the forest. From inside I look out at the water through floor-to-ceiling windows that imitate the structure of the woods outside—cedar mullions holding tall sheets of vertical light. Two trees nudge the deck, thump against it in a storm. I use them as feeding stations for birds and squirrels. A cedar pole in the center of the living room rises to support the main beam in the ceiling. I lean my back against it, put my arms around it sometimes when I am alone. I listen to the weather in the trees, the thrashing tumult they become in a high wind, the easy drip of water on the roof after a rain. From a wooden circular staircase in the back corner of the house, I look out on the first steps of the trail, let my mind climb the hill with it and take me into the forest.

Cobb Island

If you look south across Eastern Channel from the opposite shore, you won't recognize Cobb Island. It is small
and blends right in to the timbered reach of Baranof Island
behind it, appearing as a mere bump along the larger
shore. But if you go into the mouth of the bight at its east
end, your eye gets pulled to a narrow slot in the trees. That
definitive notch in the forested skyline lures you around
a corner, and the island makes itself known.

I had been looking directly at Cobb Island for years; I
could see it from my house. I had gone past it many times
and not known it was there. I discovered it the summer
I bought my boat. Those long, light-filled days offered
the best chance for exploring nearby shores. I spread my
maps out on the table and began. Many landmarks were
familiar—the Marshall Islands were right in front of the
house, Silver Bay just around a corner to the east; Bird's
Nest Cove I knew of but had not seen; Camp Coogan Bay
and Aleutkina Bay I'd been to on trips with friends. Cobb
Island caught me unaware. My surprise brought back a
line from Ezra Pound, quoted once by a graduate school
professor: "Not as land looks on a map / but as sea bord

seen by men sailing." From my living room I had that perspective—looking at sea level across the bay to the flat line of demarcation where land and water meet. Much of that shoreline seemed to have little dimension. Of course the entrances to familiar bays and inlets were easy to pick out, and a shift in the color tone of the trees might help distinguish a particular point, but the longest stretch of shore that I could see appeared unbroken, a line without dimension or form. The maps let me imagine what ought to be filled in, but even that wasn't enough. Once I was aware of Cobb Island, I knew I had to go.

My boat rides the water like a long red smile, this fourteen-foot wooden surf dory made to stand up to the Atlantic waters along the country's northeast coast. It's an unusual sight in Southeast Alaska where few people bother with boats that don't have an engine. For me, it fulfilled an old dream. For years I had wanted to have a boat that would let me relive an experience I treasured from childhood: the even stroke of oars in return for that smooth glide over water, the reciprocity of motion for motion. This boat was perfect, built specifically for rowing. The graceful lines and sturdy construction were things passed down through two centuries of Massachusetts boatbuilders. Its red paint was a more recent cheerful aberration.

The trip to Cobb Island was one of the first I made with the boat. The journey meant rowing a couple of miles south across Eastern Channel, a waterway that opens out into Sitka Sound and the Pacific Ocean. The summer days provided good rowing weather and long hours of light. I went across on a calm afternoon. Even after identifying the island on the map, I found it difficult to see it against the far shore; I simply headed in the appropriate direction. With each stroke of the oars, Pound's words ran rhythmically through my mind: *Not as land . . . looks on a map . . . but as sea bord . . . seen by men sailing.* I moved the boat out into the channel. As my position changed, the hillsides and shorelines around me shifted dimension and form. One mountain peak became visible, another disappeared; a rocky nook at water's edge flattened out while a different bight opened up and deepened. I kept checking my bearing against the far side, looking for the shift of line that would mark the island. Small swells from the ocean lifted the boat gently and eased it down while ripples gurgled at the bow. Motion for motion: my rowing was steady, the boat skimmed along.

As I neared the opposite shore, I began to hear the ravens. Their raucous commotion came from somewhere beyond the trees. I turned the boat parallel to the shore. Several bald eagles dotted the dark front of forest. One took flight and headed toward the noise. Another followed. I went after them, steering the boat around a rocky point into a small cove that lay parallel to the open channel, protected from the dominant currents and winds. The water was perfectly still. I slowed my rowing stroke, dipped the oars quietly, and let the boat glide. The ravens' cries pulled me toward the break in the trees. I eased my way around the rocks that edged the shore, turned a corner, and found myself looking down a short, narrow passage. At the other end I could see Eastern Channel widening out into Sitka Sound. *"Here* it is," I heard myself say. On my right was the southwestern shore of Cobb Island. Across from it was a finger of land attached to Baranof's mainland. Between the two, from point to point, a low bridge of rocks and sand was exposed by a low tide. In a few hours, water would cover the bridge and Cobb Island would stand on its own.

The pleasure of my small discovery made me smile. The little niche protected by Cobb Island was a lovely spot. I wondered how many times this place had been found, how many people had been lured into the cove and come around that same corner to discover the island. Discovery, the act of finding out, gaining knowledge of the unknown. "We shall not cease from exploration," says T. S. Eliot, "And the end of all our exploring / Will be to arrive where we started / And know the place for the first time."

I nosed the boat toward the short stretch of beach on my side of the bridge. The ravens fluttered noisily in the trees above, their hoarse voices scraping the air. I was closing in on the cause of their commotion. The bow of the boat eased onto the sand and I stepped out. Almost immediately there was a loud rush of wings. I turned. Eight eagles flew off down the narrow passage. The ravens' cries intensified, then faltered away and left an accusatory silence. I wished the impossible—that I were invisible, that I had muffled the loud crush of rocks and shells under my feet as I stepped ashore, as I walked slowly around the point of trees from behind which the eagles had flown—but my presence prevailed. The birds had gone. The explanation for their noisy congregation was simple: a three-and-a-half-foot salmon carcass, largely intact, lay on the beach.

I stood alone beside the fish. The beach, which sloped gently to the water, was skirted by a particular curve of hemlock and spruce. Certain rocks shaped the shore. A driftwood stump was grounded high, stranded by a storm tide. Fixtures. The things I would recognize when I came back. The things someone else would find in their own discovery of this place. But the fish—the fish seemed an anomaly. This was a secluded beach; it bridged a very narrow passage. There were no streams close by, nothing to attract a fish of this size. Anyone who had caught it would have taken it home as a prize. But its final resting place was here, in this protected spot. It was more likely to have landed almost anywhere else, but some current, some set of circumstances had put it precisely here. Its death would remain a mystery—perhaps injuries from a predator or a troller's line—but it had been delivered to this private place. The eagles and ravens found it here, as though the setting had been chosen for the ritual that marked that juncture in the life cycle of those animals—the death of one, the nourishing renewal of the others.

And then I had arrived. What had been for me a pleasurable discovery came to feel like an intrusion. I found myself embarrassed by the presumption that the landscape is mine to use any time, in any way I like. Too often I am blind to what might have been there before me, what I might see. Occasionally I am given privilege, momentary insight into the larger natural world that encompasses me. Those fleeting gifts challenge my presumption and force on me the paradox of feeling like a stranger to nature. Do I fit into this place? Do I belong?

The questions unsettled me and made me hesitant to venture far or stay long. Poking around the edge of the woods, I found the remains of a picnic—a campfire ring, pop and beer cans, styrofoam cups. The scene was easy to imagine: a small group of friends gathered around the fire for a camp meal, swapping stories or jokes, enjoying this place for its privacy and the shelter of its trees, taking advantage of the late summer light. Back out on the beach was the fish, and I thought again of the eagles congregated for their feast, the ravens hovering, waiting, the quiet cove as the setting for the event, the cycles that play themselves out in the wild. The two images pulled me in opposite directions. One took me beyond the human world, the other tied me to it. I longed for the transcendence, the feeling that I was an integral part of that place, but I was grounded with my kind. I scattered the wood of the campfire and covered the burnt scar with sand, then gathered the garbage and put it in my boat.

Before leaving, I walked the short stretch of beach on the far edge of the little bridge. The shallow water was clear and seemed to sharpen the rocks and shells just beneath its surface. Amidst them was a long thin shape, particularly white. I bent down and picked up the leg bone of a deer, absolutely clean, bleached by salt and light. I glanced around. There was another bone lying a ways away, above the tide. Hunters, I thought, the human explanation being the first to come to mind. But the bones *and* the fish—both simply washed there on the

tide? Perhaps. But what if those bones had been brought
there by some other animal? What if other creatures
sought out that place for the same seclusion and privacy
I had discovered? Why wouldn't other animals single out
favorite places in a landscape just as humans do? I have
witnessed little of the animal world, caught up as I am
in the human. I know little about other frames of mind,
preferences, reasons. But to consider those possibilities,
foreign as they are to me, let them serve as guides into the
unknown, seemed like the least I could do.

The incoming tide was about to set my boat afloat. I
climbed in, settled myself at the oars, and rowed back out
into the little cove. The channel beyond was still calm, but
riffled by a late afternoon breeze. I pulled the boat out
into open water and pointed the bow toward home. Cobb
Island was my point of reference off the stern, the even
stroke of the oars my comfort. I concentrated on the image
of that beach—rocks and shells, fish and bones, the stillness
of the air in the trees, the soft lapping of water—and imagined how the scene would come to life again when the
birds returned. I stared hard at the island as though I might
see through it, as though I could be a witness to its other
side. Instead, it disappeared, its short line of trees gradually becoming one with the longer seaboard. But it was
fixed now—an enigma, a point on a map—in my mind.

The next chance I had to return to Cobb Island was
some weeks later with a friend. Rich had wanted to see
my boat and go rowing. When he asked about a place to
go, I mentioned the island but didn't tell him why. I was
hesitant but eager to return, still uneasy about my sense

of intrusion, but pulled by the prospect of becoming more familiar with that place. I let Rich row across the channel and, as we talked, I watched that long shoreline ahead of us take shape, and signalled small moves one way or the other to keep us headed in the right direction. The summer evening light would linger almost till dawn. A bit of low chop slapped at the boat and bobbed us along. I don't remember exactly when the island became visible, but at some point I looked and could begin to make out its form. In the half hour it took us to cross, Cobb Island had completely reappeared.

The water flattened out as we pulled in to the protection of the island's little cove. The trees' reflection on the water made it look darker, deeper, glassier. The boat glided easily now. We rowed on past a small notch in the end of Cobb Island that could, from a distance, be mistaken for the break we sought in the shore. I ushered Rich on around the farther corner.

"See?" I said.

Cobb Island was truly an island this time. The tide was high enough to cover the low bridge I had found before. The quiet of the cove hushed and slowed our conversation. We rowed into the passage and watched the bottom come up to meet us as we floated over the bridge. Shells and rocks and seaweeds were given sharp clarity by the shallow water, then blurred again as the bottom fell away and darkened the water on the other side. Beyond the bridge, the shoreline of the island became a four- to eight-foot wall of steep jagged rock, as irregular as it was solid. The tide gurgled in and out of its crevices, and deep green boughs of hemlock draped low over the mosses and grasses that had planted themselves on top of the rock. We moved slowly down the passage. A light spot amidst all those dark hues caught Rich's eye.

"What's that?" he asked.

"What?" I said.

He turned the boat around and went a short way back, nosing the shore while he stood up to look. From where I was sitting, I still couldn't see what he had seen.

"It's a deer skeleton. Let me get out and look."

I took over the oars. "Again," I thought to myself. "Another death. Other bones." I nudged the boat, stern first, up against the rocks while Rich climbed out and scrambled up to a little precipice that was above the recent high tides. The skeleton was slightly disheveled, but mostly whole, and lay on a scraggly bed of moss. Would this be a place a deer might lay down to die? Had we come across evidence of the ordinary end of an animal's life? Or had its body been delivered, placed precisely there? Specifically there, in that quiet, protected spot? My mind flooded with questions and the eerie sense that, once again, I might have disturbed an intimacy. I wondered about the natural death of animals in the wild, if the occasion was a deliberately private one for them. All creatures go to death alone, but as humans we tend to acknowledge that passing in some public way. We live lives of intention, leaving behind words or deeds by which we will be remembered. Those deer bones at rest in that quiet place did not ask for such acknowledgment. They were simply part of the pattern that defines all life.

Rich and I exchanged no words as he climbed down the rocks and got back in the boat. I stayed at the oars and rowed us the length of the passage, out around the west end of Cobb Island. The strong light of day was beginning to weaken as we headed back across the channel. Rich slouched down in the stern and pretended to sleep while I established a steady motion with the oars. The island was centered off the stern. As our distance from it grew, its points of delineation faded with the light into the dark face of the larger forest. Before long, it had been absorbed again into its own backdrop. I strained my eyes to see but simply had to believe.

On my USGS topographical map, Cobb Island is a quarter-inch long and half that wide. The rocks on its east end are delineated by a squiggly line; one on its south side is marked by an asterisk. The other end of the island had been a useful reference at one time—it points north-west into Eastern Channel and is inscribed with a surveyor's benchmark. In my experience Cobb Island is at once a slight shadow on a dark wooded shore and a jagged, forested piece of rock sheltering its own quiet harbor. In my mind it is a private, dignified, peaceful, haunting place.

Eskimo people are known to have been able to produce accurate maps of their homeland working simply from memory. That ability to translate the physical landscape into an abstract one requires an intimate knowledge of the land that comes to people grounded where they live. Animals must know the land in somewhat the same way, delineating their territory, returning to familiar places again and again. Was Cobb Island marked on the interior map of some animals as it had become for me? Would I ever be able to draw the island from memory in accurate detail? If I were asked, how would I depict its mystery?

I didn't have to wait long for another quiet day to return. Curiously enough, this time the deer skeleton drew me. I wanted to go back before it was moved by the tide. I hadn't gotten out of the boat that day, hadn't climbed up the rocks myself to look—not at the details of the deer's death, but at the particulars of that structure of bones lying on their own altar of moss and stone. I needed to go again, alone. The route was easy now. I set out as I had to in my boat, my back to the island, knowing it would be visible by the time I got past the middle of the channel. *Not as land looks on a map / but as sea bord seen by men sailing*. Pound's meter once again. As distance diminished familiar houses and buildings on shore, the water and surrounding landscape took on their expansive proportions, and the boat was just large enough to sustain my belief that I was safe. I turned occasionally to look for the island's landmarks. Soon they were there, and I moved confidently across the open water.

I rowed in from the west end of the island; the tide was low and Cobb Island's bridge would have blocked my passage from the cove. I had no trouble spotting the particular niche I was looking for—there, up close to the trees. I tethered the boat precariously to the rocks below and slipped and scrambled over the mustard-colored rockweed that draped the craggy shore, holding fast to sharp edges of stone. The broken face of the island was mostly vertical, though not high. I clambered up it quickly and cautiously approached the little ledge, not certain how I would react to what I knew I would see. An exclamation of breath was all that came.

The skeleton seemed too slight to be a deer. Without the muscle and tissue that held the bones apart, the configuration had collapsed on top of itself, but its parts remained in place, nestled in its bed of grass and moss. The vertebrae of the spine were still interlocked in their intricate pattern and supported the cage of small ribs that had housed the deer's lungs and heart, the nucleus of breath and blood. At the top of the spine lay the skull, its complex structure of bone plates delineated by the delicate seams that zigzagged across it. The lower jaw had been separated, but its long graceful curve still held the deer's teeth. The perfect ovals of the eye sockets were both lovely and eerie, their structure a tribute to natural form, their emptiness the most vivid sign of the life that was gone. Bits of hair still clung to the bone and were scattered over the rock's covering of lichen and moss. Otherwise, the bones were clean, tinged pink in places with the lifeblood they had held. Other animals had been here, had been nourished by that deer's life, had played their part in the return of that life to the earth.

I didn't stay long. The boat needed tending, but that was an excuse. The poignancy made me falter: that small body in that private place, its testimony to the ultimate sacrifice at the heart of life, to the grace that gives us form and sustains us, that dwells on after us, even in our bones.

I climbed back down to the boat and rowed over for

a walk on the short stretch of beach between Cobb and Baranof Islands. Other deer bones were scattered about: a jaw with all but four or five teeth gone; knuckled rings of vertebrae, some torn loose, others whose ligaments still held them together; a slender tibia from a lower leg. Some had been in saltwater awhile, were bleached white and studded with limpets and snails. Others were still pink at the core, still closer to life than they were to the decay of death. What made this little enclave such a repository? What might I witness if I could keep an invisible watch? What was I inhibiting by my presence? I walked a bit in the fringe of the forest. My untrained eye found few clues except some clam and abalone shells left, perhaps, by raven or otter. Another campfire had been built high on the beach, the remains of another picnic left behind. I scattered the scorched pieces of wood and collected the beer cans. Such traces were part of a human story laid down on top of the one told by the place itself. I longed to know those other plots, those other characters, but these would have to be their own discoveries, revealed over time.

I lifted the bow of the boat and pushed it back into the water, shoving off with one foot as I climbed in with the other, then settling myself and letting the boat drift in silence. A slight wake rippled away across the glassy surface of the water and burbled against Cobb Island's broken wall of stone. From high in the trees came the faint chipping of small birds. I dipped the oars and pulled away from the beach, down the narrow passage, back toward the west end of the island. I looked up at the ledge of rock where the skeleton lay and caught just a glimpse of white. A squirrel let go a nervous rattle from a nearby tree. "I'm going, I'm going," I thought in reply. I rounded the end of the island and pulled the boat toward home. That small outcrop of forested rock was the center of my view, and I imagined the inhabitants of its secluded cove resuming their activities while I moved farther and farther away. Neither land as it looks on a map nor sea bord as seen by men sailing. I let Cobb Island disappear against the larger shore, and held in mind its rocks and beach and trees; its deaths, its quiet waters; the pieces of skeleton, pink and white, the spirit that colors our bones.

Centering Place

Perhaps it wasn't the most romantic of beginnings. I was struggling to respond to Dorik's questions about liberation theology while I sipped sherry and he scotch. It was our first evening out, and we were finishing it off with a nightcap in the lounge at the top of the Captain Cook Hotel in Anchorage. The atmosphere was right—lights low, some soft jazzy music, a spread of windows that looked out over that northern metropolis in the rose-gold summer twilight. A bowl of mountains cradled the city and Cook Inlet, which stretched off to the west before it turned south. Looking north, the urban lights faded into the open expanse that showed off Mount McKinley on a clear day, two hundred miles inland. We'd spent a roundabout day in the country that now stretched out around us, driving first down to Portage Glacier south of Anchorage, and then back north through the city and out to Wasilla to have dinner at Dorik's oldest daughter's restaurant. When we returned to town, neither of us was willing to end the day, so we stopped and rode the elevator to the Captain Cook's penthouse lounge. Quite a few other people shared the place with us, but I doubted any

of them were discussing liberation theology. My willingness to engage Dorik, in spite of my ignorance, wasn't
mere posturing. I was intrigued. Here was a mind that
shared my fascination for ideas, that was grounded outside popular American culture. We hadn't stopped talking
all day, and sensed, perhaps, that there was a lifetime of
conversation out in front of us. Another sherry, another
scotch, and we left the theologians behind.

The story that captured my imagination was the remarkable one of how Dorik's parents had settled in the
small community of Redstone, Colorado, a place that
became the family home. When Frank and Paula Mechau
took some visitors up the Crystal River valley to Redstone
for a picnic on a summer day in 1936, they fully expected
the deserted coal-mining company town that they found.
There were the workers' houses, no two alike, neatly
laid out along the community's single main street; the
idle coke ovens lined up at the mouth of Coal Basin; the
worker's club house; the stately Redstone Inn; and just
a mile further up the valley, the owner's mansion, well
accompanied by the appropriate accoutrements that befit
a gentleman of John Cleveland Osgood's fortune—a gate-
house, carriage house and stables, dog kennels, a green-
house, and an ice house. Osgood was the founder and
principal stockholder of Colorado Fuel and Iron Company.
Redstone was his dream, a model company town that
provided work for people who could live decently because their employer treated them decently. A politically
conservative businessman, Osgood wanted to avoid any
sympathies with the new and growing organized labor

movement. In the best paternalistic fashion, he made sure
his workers were well taken care of. Each of their cottages
was distinct—particular architectural features and paint
a different color than the house next door. They were
comfortable places to live. And after a tiring day's work
tending the coke ovens, the workers retired to the club
house where they could shower and leave their dirty work
clothes in lockers, have a drink, and perhaps play a game
of billiards before going home to their families. Or they
could browse through books and magazines—in several
languages—in the library that was available to all members of the community. The contented workers would
help Osgood expand his fortune. The mine up Coal Basin
offered plenty of coal for the coking operation that would
create fuel to fire the company's steel mill across the state
in Pueblo. And he, John C. Osgood, could have the pleasure of watching it all from his luxuriant quarters just
upriver in this magnificent mountain valley. It must have
been a good life while it lasted, a short six or seven years
at the turn of the century. Osgood's Redstone enterprise
came to an end when he lost his principalship in the
company. His consolation, useless as it was with no economic backbone, was ownership of the community and
estate he had created for himself.

Frank Mechau had grown up in Glenwood Springs, a
town just thirty miles north of Redstone, and he'd heard
many a story about Osgood's failed enterprise. He assumed
he was taking his visitors to a ghost town on that summer
day, and the place was virtually deserted. But when they
stopped at the Redstone Inn to take a look at its handsome

clock tower, they were surprised to be greeted by an African-American man in a starched white jacket who invited them in for lunch. Inside were Osgood's third wife and widow, who had remarried and was now Mrs. MacDonald; her sister; and one other person. The Mechau party joined them, and while they chatted over lunch, Mrs. MacDonald let on that individual houses in Redstone were for sale. There was one, in fact, she thought might suit them. Paula convinced Frank they should at least go and see what it was like, though they were hardly in a position to buy a house. It was, after all, the 1930s. People in Colorado, like Americans everywhere, were feeling the effects of the Depression. And Frank was trying to make a living as an artist, a painter. He and Paula were raising a family. Financially, they were just getting by.

Still, the Crystal River valley was an enchanting place, folded into the western slope of the Colorado Rockies. The valley floor narrowed as it went upriver, and Redstone was located in a canyon framed by steep red rock cliffs. Five creeks came down out of the upper reaches of the backcountry to join the Crystal in that stretch of the canyon. On up the river to the south, Chair Mountain and Ragged Mountain loomed over aspen-covered hillsides. Blue spruce and ponderosa pine mottled those forests with dark contrast. To the north, down valley, the high slopes and sharp peak of Mount Sopris dominated the landscape. Overhead, more often than not, the skies were a sharp high-altitude blue.

After lunch, Mrs. MacDonald showed the Mechaus the house she had in mind. It was a two-story home that offered ample room for the family. The price was eighteen hundred dollars. They didn't have that much money but were captivated by the idea of living in Redstone—so much so that within a week they had scraped together enough for a down payment. They were soon to be one of the first families to move into Redstone after John Osgood's demise.

The Mechau family adventure of living in that mountain refuge was a high-spirited one. That was clear from the spark in Dorik's eyes as he talked. His love of the place permeated the quiet sureness of his voice and the clarity of his telling. His father's success as an artist had periodically pulled the family away from Redstone, but they always returned as soon as they could, enthusiastically each time, as though it were the only place on earth where they belonged. Seven years after their move to Redstone, they made a trade of their first house plus five hundred dollars for a house two miles upriver from the village, a house Osgood had lived in while his mansion was being built, a house quickly filled with the Mechaus' second phase of Crystal River stories and visitors and good times. Those days were tragically altered just three years later when Frank Mechau's heart suddenly stopped at the age of forty-two. Dorik's mother, brother, and two sisters bound themselves together around that anguish, and though they had to make several temporary moves so that Paula could work, the house in Redstone held fast as the centering place. The Crystal River valley was irreplaceable, the touchstone for their lives.

That story was more than enough to enchant my second glass of sherry. I listened with both heart and mind, recognizing elements of a sensibility I ached to be able to call my own: knowing a landscape like the back of my hand, knowing a place that was lodged deeply enough that it pulled my life into focus, knowing the continuity of a life lived from childhood through middle age with the linked and constant center points of place and family. Lucky man, I remember thinking. How seldom our childhood ground stays secure. How much more often our young hearts first break with those leave-takings we cannot influence or change. With good fortune and will our families hold, but the primary rootedness that affects how steadily we walk in the world is too often a loss never recovered.

The evening at the Captain Cook didn't take long to grow into a comfortably enticing tangle. Dorik was living in Anchorage, filling in as director of the Alaska Humanities Forum. I was in Sitka running a small non-profit organization that incorporated the arts and humanities into programs focused on literature and human values. Our jobs had introduced us, and now that we knew we had plenty to talk about, our long-distance phone bills started climbing. The more weeks went by, the more the after-dinner phone calls became expected. One evening Dorik startled me by asking if I'd like to take a trip to Mexico with him. He could get a good deal on airfares if he bought two hundred dollars worth of merchandise at Kmart—things, of course, that he really needed, like socks and odds and ends of kitchenware and . . . he was sure he could find something. I stammered a bit while he explained, but when I answered yes, I knew things had turned a corner. We never took that south-of-the-border journey but still use a couple of aluminum frying pans that were part of his shopping spree.

Our first trip together was, instead, to the Crystal River valley for Thanksgiving. By that time Dorik's family and I had become intriguing prospects to each other. They were all curious and delighted with the idea that I might put an end to the various failed matchmaking attempts they had made during the ten years since the breakup of Dorik's first marriage. His second daughter, Mally, who lived across country, was unable to contain her inquisitiveness and schemed a way to show up on the scene as a surprise. And his mother was pleased and eager. "Well," she said our first evening there, when I was on the other side of the door, "have you asked her?" I was welcomed virtually without question.

And there I was in the Mechau home celebrated in Dorik's tales. The details of his stories began to place themselves: his father's paintings and drawings hanging in almost every room—early abstractions and the later horses and Colorado landscapes that came to characterize his work. The long dining-room table and benches his father built had hosted many a festive dinner. The coal cookstove in his mother's kitchen had gathered everyone around its warmth. The push-button light switches from Osgood's time were still functional. The upstairs boys' bedroom was much like it was when Dorik had huddled on winter nights between cold sheets, waiting for his small-boy warmth to spread itself into the bedcovers. Out the back door, there were the red rock cliffs studded with spruce and pine and the high aspened ridges where his father had taken him hunting and taught him to use his first rifle. And below the house was the murmuring Crystal River, clear as its name, that collected rainbow trout and mountain water from Hayes Creek and Kline, Hawk Creek and East and Coal, each with its beaver ponds or sandstone falls or thirst-quenching pools or bouldered rubble.

When my parents first met Dorik, I made him tell them the Redstone story, certain that it would charm them. The story had its effect, but wasn't quite enough for my father who, some months later when he and Dorik were both in Sitka for an annual symposium that I organized, took him to lunch to ask him his intentions. Dorik made it clear that his intentions were nothing but honorable, that I was the only one posing a question. In a more playful way, my father took up a similar question with Mally, who had come for the symposium as well. How did she feel about *his* daughter capturing the heart of *her* father? I don't know what Mally said to my father, but she had already answered the question in a poem that had won her first place in a statewide competition.

Finding Words

My deskbound father
is in love with a woman
from Sitka. She called him
Sunday afternoon, looking out
through broad panes of glass
down to the dark waters of her cove.

"The whales are breaching," she told him.

When he calls me in Homer
I bring the telephone to the window.
Across the bay one patch of light
illumines the ice field. And I
show him I welcome his new love
by speaking her strange dialect.

"The glacier is calving," I tell him.

While everyone waited for my decision, Dorik left
his job in Anchorage and moved to Sitka. Over weeks
and months, the view of the waters beyond those broad
panes of glass grew to be his as well as mine, the breaching whales a shared marvel. One evening, standing in
our narrow kitchen passage between the washer/dryer
and refrigerator, I faced him and answered yes.

We let the word out slowly, casually, reserving its
moment for ourselves. When it came time to decide
on a place to host a ceremony and family celebration,
my first love beckoned. The ocean. A friend of a friend
recommended a small community on the Oregon coast,
and we made arrangements long distance, sight unseen,

for a weekend of merrymaking that gave sweet blessing to one of the most courageous days and happy hours of our lives.

A favorite wedding gift arrived in the mail after we returned to Sitka. It came from the Fenders, Colorado ranchers and longtime Mechau family friends that I had yet to meet. Pat had sent a kind note with a check. "Buy yourselves a photo album," she suggested, "but if that doesn't suit you, buy some beef." I was charmed by this spiritedness: it bespoke no ordinary friendship. And Dorik's Fender stories were laced with fondness and admiration. Pat was a Vassar graduate who had come west to work as a teacher, a tall beauty who caught the attention of more than one ranching cowboy. Long lean Bill Fender, handsome from hat to boot, won out. He and his brothers were running the old Fender ranch, one of the larger private landholdings in the Crystal River valley. It spread itself out on some of the higher mesas and slopes that flanked Mount Sopris, downriver from Redstone. With passing years, the Fender brothers came to inherit the ranch along with its challenges—the difficulty of managing that much land and livestock for a profit, the brothers' divergent interests that weren't necessarily devoted to ranching, and, in due time, the early development pressures that signaled the unsettling of the valley as it had once been known. Ranches had laid out the primary pattern of occupancy—wide open hay meadows and pastures bounded by a creek bank or mountain slope or rail fence that bordered another ranch. On an edge or corner of the land a house shaded with cottonwoods or aspens, the associated barn and sheds nestled nearby. Each place with its corrals and its loading chute for both cattle and horses. Almost always a dirt lane that led visitors to a front porch. But the predominant feature was the quiet reach of the valley, uncluttered, protected by its unwelcoming potholed and rutted dusty narrow roads, contained by the close and steep rise of the high summits that marched along the westward face of the Rockies, the continent's backbone.

That was the valley Dorik loved. That was the reach of land that spread across the canvases of his father's paintings. On each of my early visits, Dorik's memories sketched out more details. There was the old Grubb ranch that the Perrys, other longtime family friends, had bought. That piece too, the one that rested against the foothills, was theirs. As we made our way upriver and the valley narrowed, the larger ranches became cor- respondingly smaller—patchworked acres that fit them- selves onto whatever ground was tenable. Ranch hand Roy Hungerford's place was on an east-facing hillside looking up Avalanche Creek, which runs along the base of Mount Sopris. There was the site of the tiny shack, across the road and river from the hot springs, where Uriah McLean used to live with Bertha, who he always claimed was his cousin, not his wife. Near his place was the spot where Valuable Dust, a gold-mining optimist, had camped each summer when he came to soak his rheumatism in those heated waters. Most people didn't have much money. Land was relatively cheap, but making a living on it wasn't easy. A person like Uriah had a cow, perhaps. Some chickens. Maybe a garden in the summer. With luck, a hunted deer or elk from the high country. And the people themselves were few. Down valley, the town of Carbondale might have been home to a couple hundred, not counting ranchers. The further upriver you went, the thinner the population. When the Mechaus moved to Redstone, the only other families in the village were the Kenneys and the Claytons, both caretakers of the Osgood legacy, and the Monteveres, who had the pieced-together ranch just south of town. Dorik remembers a weathered billboard at the entrance to Redstone that anyone coming up valley would notice. "2- AND 3-ROOM COTTAGES FOR SALE. $250 AND $300." The sign drew little interest. Not many people bothered to drive the chuckholed road to see it, and most wouldn't have considered living in such an out of the way place. For Dorik, that place and its surrounding valley was a sanctuary.

The Redstone billboard, of course, is long gone. Its disappearance was a harbinger of the unsettling that began after World War II when the country's prosperity started to find its way into scenic western hideaways like the Crystal River valley. People in Redstone began to notice the change after Walter Paepke, a monied visionary, discovered the town of Aspen on the Roaring Fork, the river in the watershed just east of the Crystal. Paepke dreamed of making Aspen into a western mecca of high culture. He found it relatively easy to acquire property by paying off delinquent taxes, and soon owned enough of the town to be able to establish an institute for humanistic studies with associated music festivals and artist conclaves. Paepke's vision coincided with others' who were keen on making Aspen a ski resort. The combination of the two did, indeed, bring people, and they came by way of Carbondale, where the Roaring Fork meets the Crystal, where the spur road branches off to Redstone. Many ignored that turn-off, but others didn't, and it wasn't long before the proper authorities deemed it a good idea to pave the Crystal River road. Nothing up that valley beckoned quite like Aspen, but the more convenient access piqued both interest and curiosity. Though change came more slowly, it came—new houses along the river, different property owners in Redstone, regular traffic along the road, bigger ranches like the Fenders' subdivided and sold to developers.

Dorik had witnessed this gradual transformation during summers home from college. He witnessed more changes every time he visited after marriage and various jobs took him out of the valley. He chronicled those changes to me before he ever drove me up the Crystal River road to the Redstone home. The landscape stunned me the first time I saw it, and I watched it bring a deep smile of recognition to Dorik's eyes, but I knew his memories were of a wholeness that was no longer there. I realized that he held a kind of perspective and knowledge that has been lost over and over again in the settlement of the continent, over and over again in the civilization of the world.

A couple years after my first Redstone visit we learned, while talking on the phone with Dorik's brother, that the Perrys had decided to sell off a big piece of their ranch to a developer who wanted to put in a golf course. The story was confirmed when we received an issue of *High Country News,* a regional biweekly paper focused on the complex issues of growth in the west. The Perry sale was highlighted as an example, the story's headline zeroing in on one of the painful human dilemmas that accompanies this kind of change: "Golf Course Splits Ranch Family." The article put the details in a nutshell. A rancher ready to retire and finding it easier to equitably divide cash between his heirs rather than land. A daughter interested in slowing growth, preserving viable ranches, and protecting their owners from the rising property taxes most likely to accompany this development. Burgeoning Aspen, only a half hour away, overflowing its bounds and driving Carbondale prime agricultural land up to luxury prices of fifteen thousand dollars and more per acre. The golf course and three other proposed developments increasing the town's population of thirty-one hundred more than twofold.

Dorik shook his head slowly as he read the story. I watched his face tighten and knew that a deepening ache was filling him. Places and people he loved were both caught in the wake of rampant development that grew like a cancer. The impact was like a diagnosis of the disease itself, as though one of the most fundamental aspects of his life was being eaten away. I wondered then about the grief that comes to us when we lose places we love. This grief doesn't have much standing among the range of human emotions that our society values. We have yet to fully acknowledge and accept just how much our hearts are entwined with the places that shape us, tolerate us, hold us, provide for us. We have yet to openly testify and accede to the necessity of such places and love of them in our everyday lives. We have yet to fully understand that our links as people living together in communities will never be more than transient and vulnerable without a rootedness in place itself.

When Dorik and I made our next visit to the Crystal River valley, huge earth-moving machines were hard at work in Carbondale, shaping the ranch land to conveniently accommodate the boxy homes that accompanied the golf course—lower-priced ones nearer the road, custom luxury models closer to the groomed green expanse that would serve as a stand-in for a more natural landscape. The scene silenced us both. We drove on up the road to Redstone without speaking of what we had just seen, as though we could hold off its truth if we could avoid giving it words. But the ache that needled its way into both our hearts was inescapable. Upriver, the red rock and high valley walls seemed to offer sanctuary, but there on the mesa across from town was the spreading new home of a retired architect. And there, below the Mechau house, was the expanding compoundlike enclave belonging to successful entrepreneurs who crafted chic chandeliers and furniture out of deer and elk antlers. Up the hill behind the house, lots had been sold and houses built on the slopes storied with Dorik's hunting trips and hiking adventures.

Walking through the back door into the family kitchen we found refuge. Dorik's mother's arms and smile embraced us. She had a coal fire burning in the woodstove. The room was warm. Brueghel's *Wedding Feast* hung where it had for years above the oak table. The linoleum floor was scuffed and worn from patterns of family habit. Coal buckets sat in their place beside the stove, worn pot holders hung in theirs on a rack above. The cupboards and counter top and wainscoting were nicked and speckled with use, with the weeks and months and seasons of people gathering to share meals and stories and spirited talk in that room. High on a set of corner shelves was a 1930s photograph of Frank Mechau. Below it was a framed postcard of one of his paintings. *Tom Kenney Comes Home* depicts a weather-worn cowhand, miner, and friend, broad brimmed hat cocked on his head, red bandanna tied round his neck. He is on horseback, paused on a mountain ledge beside a gnarled and reaching snag, perhaps returning from a mining expedition, a string of three tired and loaded horses behind him. Out in front of him, a golden evening sky spreads behind the bare flanks of Mount Sopris. But Tom's gaze is focused below. In the lee of that mountain, resting quietly against its slopes, the familiar reach of the valley, silent and serene, beckons and welcomes him home.

In our own kitchen on the shores of Thimbleberry Bay in Sitka, Dorik regaled me one evening with stories about Tom Kenney and his brother John. Tom worked wherever and at whatever he could—a ranch or two here and there in season, a mining prospect when the luck was right. John was senior caretaker of the Osgood properties in Redstone. He wore his long underwear year-round and buttoned his shirt collars tight around his neck. His wife, Norma, was the schoolteacher. As a boy Dorik spent many summer days tagging along with John as he made his work rounds and patiently showed Dorik the details of useful skills like sharpening a knife or fixing a pipe. Tom would come and stay with John and Norma now and then, and each time he did, Norma would demand that he take a bath. When Dorik's father finished *Tom Kenney Comes Home,* he took a photograph of it to Tom, who studied it a few minutes and then said, "That's pretty good, Frank."

For the moment, the Crystal River valley had come alive again in Dorik's eyes. But then his smile saddened. The stories silenced him. We both turned away. Outside our windows the water flickered. Cedar tree boughs quivered in an easy breeze. The forested mountains across the bay stood their silent watch. Gulls wheeled in the distance, their white wings flecking the dark slopes and the gray sky. Dorik opened the kitchen door and stepped out. I watched him walk slowly along the deck, taking in deep breaths of the sea-forest air. When he came back inside, we sat down to a fresh king salmon dinner. His chair faced the window, and his eyes roamed the new landscape that had taken hold in his heart. "Thanks for this place," he said.

In Good Hands at Sea

If you get caught at sea in a storm in a dory, lie down in the bottom of the boat. It might scare you to death, but you'll never get drowned out there." Such was the advice of Frederick "Tink" Lowell, fifth in a family line of seven generations of boat builders who owned the oldest boat manufacturing shop in the United States. Lowell's Boat Shop made the dory moored outside my house. I try to keep those words of advice in mind anytime I'm out in the boat. Being a bit of a nervous sailor, I pick my weather as best I can, but it's comforting to know that I have a reliable little craft for those fickle moods of sky. It's all the more reassuring to know that Lowell's dories have been trusted for over two hundred years.

I first saw my boat tied up in a Sitka harbor. I spotted it from the sidewalk on the bank above the water, and made a detour down to the dock to take a closer look. That particular harbor float was lined with small boats, most of them aluminum skiffs, Boston Whalers and some small cabined fiberglass boats. In the middle of the lineup was a wooden dory, clear varnish on its golden pine planks, dark mahogany seats, a neatly coiled line in its bow. It floated on the water like a beautiful bowl fit to the slender leaf-shape of its double-pointed base. Four planks on each side, tacked one above the other, curved out gently to define the dory's four-foot beam, and back in to meet the rise of the bow stem forward and the sharp triangular transom in the stern. If I cup my hands, keeping my fingertips together, I can almost recreate its shape.

I'd like to think Simeon Lowell might have cupped his hands in the same way when he thought about the design for these boats two centuries ago. He was forty-eight years old when he built a boat shop in 1793 on three quarters of an acre at Salisbury Point on the Merrimack River in Amesbury, Massachusetts. The place is now known as Point Shore in Amesbury, and Lowell's Boat Shop is still there and still producing wooden boats, many a dory among them. Simeon Lowell was a descendent of mariners and boat builders. Some of the first boats he built were dories like mine, flat-bottomed rowboats with rounded lapstrake sides and a V-shaped transom. Local and family legend attributes the design to Simeon himself, a modification of a boat called a wherry that was widely used by New Englanders of the time to get around on the rivers and shores. The design changes made the small boats more seaworthy and they soon became popular with fishermen up and down the coast.

Another later modification created the Banks dory, an easier-to-build lightweight boat with straighter sides that allowed the dories to be stacked one inside another on the decks of halibut schooners that fished the Grand Banks in the mid and late nineteenth century. When at sea, the dories were lowered to the water with a crew of one or two who fished the day, brought their catch back to the schooner, hoisted their boat up on deck for the night, and lowered it again to fish again in the morning. The Banks dory kept Lowell's Boat Shop in business until technological changes in the fishing industry made the use of dories less efficient and not as lucrative. By the 1930s a growing demand for recreational boats kept the shop in business, and that popular pastime still requires the boatbuilders at Lowell's to hone their skills. Simeon's descendants, including Tink, carried on what became a legendary business and tradition.

I can't help but wonder if Simeon had any notion that he was starting something that would continue for more than two centuries. He could not have known that his boat shop would become a national historic landmark. If he could have had any inkling of what the world would be like at the end of the twentieth century, he would undoubtedly feel a great satisfaction in knowing that the shop and business he started not only remains dedicated to the craft of building fine wooden boats, but also is educating the public about traditional boatbuilding techniques.

My dory was made at Lowell's in 1983, commissioned by a man named Jan Payne, a Navy commander stationed at a submarine base in Groton, Connecticut. The original receipt for the boat tells part of the story. He visited the boat shop in August of that year and came back less than a month later with his truck to pick up a fourteen-foot surf dory. The boat was unpainted when he got it, and he had asked to have it rigged with rowing blocks for thole pins rather than oarlocks. The sticker price: $2,180. Over a year later, he ordered a pair of maple oars for the boat from the noted Shaw and Tenney oar manufacturers in Maine. Some kind of a break in his Navy service gave him the time to haul the boat all the way across the country and put it in the water in Southeast Alaska. The embarkation point I heard about was the little fishing town of Pelican on northwest Chichagof Island. How he got from the mainland to Pelican I don't know, but from there he rowed south along the outside coast of West Chichagof, across Salisbury Sound to Baranof Island, and on down to Sitka.

I hadn't quite acknowledged my dream of having such a boat of my own until I saw this one. It was the first boat in Sitka that I coveted, and I visited it often. I knew nothing of its history then, but it was just my size and speed. I'd not had a lot of experience with boats, but one of my fondest and most physical memories was of learning to row when I was a young girl. I walked back and forth along the dock beside the dory and could feel my bones and muscles remember the movement of rowing—the forward stretch, the pull of oar blade against water, the boat's corresponding forward glide, and the rhythmic repetition: stroke and stroke and stroke. Somebody else in Sitka appreciated the pleasure of that simplicity. In a small town it's not hard to find out what belongs to whom, and I soon discovered that the boat's owner was a woman I knew. When my envy became apparent, she just smiled knowingly. She had bought the boat from Jan Payne after he had made the trip from Pelican to Sitka.

The dory's slip was one I could see any time I walked past the harbor. Amidst all the trollers, longliners, seiners, and smaller fishing boats, it stood out because of its lack of equipment—nets, buoys, trolling gear and lines, gas tanks, outboard engine, gaff hooks, cooler, radar, downriggers were all absent. The dory was in fact rather plain, its structure bared for all to see. And yet it was an exquisite piece of craftsmanship. Its historic lineage as a working fishing boat wasn't evident except to aficionados who could look at its design and know its seaworthiness. One winter it disappeared for a stretch of several weeks. Afraid it had been sold out of town, I asked and was reassured to know it just needed some maintenance. When the dory reappeared, it had a thick coat of scarlet red paint. How *could* you, I thought. But my sense of sacrilege gradually gave way to the boat's inherent charm. The red paint brought out its more jaunty personality.

Several years later a friend mentioned there was a Lowell dory for sale in town. At that point, I didn't know a Lowell dory from any other kind, but when he told me where it was moored I knew precisely which boat it was. It had been sold one more time since application of the red paint, but the current owners were also acquaintances of mine. They had enjoyed the boat but wanted something a bit bigger, a skiff with an outboard that would make it easier to get around. I tussled uselessly with all the questions one should ask before making such an investment. Friends whose advice I sought knew before I did—and before any money changed hands—that the dory was as good as mine.

On a sunny June day, my friend Lauren and I launched my little red boat from the harbor float with a commemorative bottle of sparkling cider. I got myself used to the oars as we maneuvered our way past all the other boats. Once we cleared the harbor breakwater, I could get a feel for the particular stroke that moved the boat with ease. A slight afternoon breeze riffled the inner reaches of Sitka Sound and the water lapped playfully at the bow. Lauren grinned at me from the stern seat. She knew how happy I was.

I had never gone home from town by way of the water before. The road and shoreline I traveled and looked out from each day were changed by that reversal in point of view. Already I understood that the boat was going to afford me a new familiarity with this place I thought I knew. My ignorance was right at the surface that day. We passed islands I hadn't noticed from shore. We hesitated at the entrance to passages I wasn't sure would allow us through to where we needed to go. I thought it wisest to stay wide of them all for this first trip, to move out a bit and simply parallel the shoreline all the way home. There would be plenty of other opportunities. For a brief moment, I had a keen sense of the nature of the decisions early explorers had to make on their first ventures along this coast. Every opening is a lure, every headland offers a new beyond.

I live on Thimbleberry Bay, a fairly protected place to moor a boat. The bay is sheltered by the two Marshall Islands that separate it from the open reach of Eastern

Channel, a straight lead out to the North Pacific. A southerly gale can make Thimbleberry look more like that ocean, but most often the winds go by in an easterly or westerly direction and the water inside the islands stays relatively calm. The shoreline is mostly rocky and steep, but there's a curve of sloping beach that begins a bit east of our house and offers easy access to the water. Just a ways offshore there, the bottom becomes sandy and hosts a small bed of eelgrass at just the right depth and distance from the rocks to put an anchor and mooring buoy for the boat. Another friend offered to place them for me. He hoisted a netted bundle of boulders over the side of his skiff and left a bright pink tethered buoy floating on the surface. I would use an inflatable Avon raft to get out there from the beach. This spot would be the dory's new home.

Having the boat changed the view I looked at every day. The landscape came alive with possibilities. The shore across Eastern Channel felt like a new neighborhood, the water itself became an expansive front yard. I now had a way to get there, to be in the midst of that scene. Long summer days offered plenty of chances, and the dory and I kept good company. Sometimes I rowed out just to sit on the water and feel the constant pulse of its undulations. Or I would go the distance across the channel and snug the boat up close to the shore to see what was living on the tidal rocks, to watch the sway of seaweed in the wash of dark water over starfish and barnacles. On the spur of the moment I would pack a light supper—fruit, crackers, cheese, and wine—and go find

a new place in a cove or inlet to have a floating picnic. I
drifted among phalaropes, watching their skittish flight
and spinning dance on the water. I rowed out to get a
closer view of whales. Cormorants and gulls flew low
over the boat. A curious seal would follow in my wake,
or a group of sea lions bob their whiskered snouts up
beside me. Some evenings, I would take the boat out into
the middle of the channel to watch the day's last flare of
light across the western sky. Sometimes I couldn't help
but lift my voice in song.

People got used to seeing that bright spot of red out on
the water. I went often to visit friends who lived on an island out from town. It was a three-mile row to their place,
most of it a clear shot across the open Eastern Channel.
They could see me coming from a long way off and came
to welcome me when I got within talking distance. There
were many late evenings after a fine meal when I would
row back home in the dark. That stretch of water felt more
private then, as though the darkness brought everything
close. Still, there was plenty to give me bearing. I could
usually make out the shapes of the mountains against the
midnight sky, and a necklace of lights outlined the Sitka
shore, thinning out as it reached away from town. Out in
the channel a navigational marker flashed and lit up the
dory's red dazzle as we passed. Sometimes the trip home
felt like a stealthy one—a little boat with no engine and no
lights, gliding quietly across the night water. Other boats
announced themselves from a long ways off—the whine
of an outboard on a speeding skiff or the chugging engine
of a tug with its three vertical running lights signaling a

load in tow. The skipper of one such boat caught the slight wake of the dory in his headlight one night and searched all over the channel until he found me, half a mile off, pulling contentedly at the oars. He shone that spot on me for several long minutes, as though he couldn't quite make out what he was seeing. But more often than not, I had that stretch of water to myself. One clear night I was particularly lucky. A fall coolness had chilled the air and the sky was strewn with stars. The channel was calmed by long smooth ocean swells that the dory rode with ease. My stroke was effortless and even, an unneeded yet welcome comfort. I didn't want to get home. Two-thirds of the way across the channel we began to move through patches of phosphorescence. The oars lit up the water as though they had brought the stars down out of the sky. The dripping backstroke created a glowing arc along each side of the boat, and the bow pushed back a glitter of small waves. In glassy spots I could see the Great Bear reflected in the water beside me. As I pulled in behind the Marshall Islands, a gossamer aurora began to streak the eastern sky, shimmering pale green scarves of light waving elusively across the face of heaven. I slowed my stroke and lingered toward anchor, blessing the night and the dory for this witness.

Over and over again, the little red boat has afforded me such gifts, things I would never see from my comfortable but landlocked place on the shore. I have never ventured far—three miles west, five miles north, up to the end of a nearby bay, into the back reaches of a hidden cove. The land is always within view, always a source of certainty. The dory itself is my safety, as much as anyone can have such while at sea. I think of Simeon Lowell and imagine the implicit trust he must have had in the design of this little craft. I think of mariners throughout human time who have wagered their lives on the reliability of yachts, schooners, trollers, skiffs, canoes, *baidarkas,* brigs, umiaks, *pangas,* sloops, junks, freighters, or seiners. I remember a photograph of the *Bernice A,* the boat my father worked on for a Southeast Alaska fishing season in the 1930s. I wonder if he was ever frightened on that trip. Or seasick. I remember him reassuring me in my young nervousness about tipsy rowboats. I remember him sitting beside me, teaching me the basic rowing stroke, holding one oar while my small hands held the other, letting me feel for myself the principles of that motion. Perhaps he recalled those days as fondly as I did on the evening I called from Sitka to ask if he and my mother could help me buy the dory. A short time later he sent me a note card his mother had given to him. "Dear God," it says, "be good to me. The sea is so wide and my boat is so small."

When I began to assume the tasks of taking care of my little wooden boat, I called Lowell's Boat Shop to ask some questions. They were delighted to hear that one of their dories was plying the waters of Southeast Alaska. I thought perhaps mine was one of the few of their boats that had ventured so far from its birthplace, but found out that Lowell dories had been sold around the world for many years. Fishermen respected and trusted these legendary boats and depended on them for their livelihood. Other people apparently did too. Perhaps the most interesting account is of Donald B. MacMillan, a 1930s Arctic explorer, who found a Lowell dory pulled up on an ice floe when he was returning from an expedition. He welcomed that sign of civilization and tracked down the shop to order several more boats for subsequent trips to the north. The more I found out, the more I respected and trusted my own Lowell. It had proven itself once when a friend and I had been caught by a fast-moving weather front that changed a calm sunny day into a passing gale. And it cinched my allegiance when a January storm flipped it over at anchor. I worried about it all night, but couldn't get to it until the next morning when the storm had subsided. When Dorik and I rowed out to it in the Avon, we found it floating assuredly upside down, all its seats and stays and bailers and buoys contained inside its canvas cover. We managed to get the cover off and retrieve all those pieces before some friends arrived with their bigger boat to help us right it. The dory rolled over with ease, submerged but suspended by its own buoyancy, its gunwales barely above the surface. I pumped and bailed that winter water without putting on any gloves. My hands, which easily numb with cold, were not the least bit chilled.

I recently hauled the dory out to give it a new coat of bottom paint. After I had cleared it of a healthy growth of mussels, barnacles, and seaweed, scraped some paint, and let it dry a day or two, I noticed there were quite a few little cracks that were seeping water. The previous owners had patched some dinged spots and those were oozing too. Some of my own rockier adventures had left nicks and gouges. The closer I looked the more it began to sink in: my planned two-day schedule for painting and taking advantage of high tides would have to be put aside. I called Lowell's again to get details of what I knew was a layered hull construction. Epoxy over a single sheet of fiberglass cloth laid down on the wood, I was told. Open up the cracks and sand them down to bare wood. For the rest of the hull, just take off the epoxy. Put some heat lamps on it to get it all good and dry, then refill the cracks with an epoxy putty. And then you can put a fresh layer of epoxy over the whole hull before you paint.

That phone call extended the maintenance job into weeks. It was early fall, the season when Sitka racks up a good number of its one hundred inches of annual rain. Humidity levels were at their usual high, air temperatures were cool. No boat that had been sitting in the water for a year was going to dry very quickly. Besides all that, Dorik and I had lots of other work to do. But our neighbors had a workshop on the shore and were willing to share its space. We sanded off the first layers of old paint while the boat was on the beach, then moved it inside to work in earnest. The electric sander's gritty whine droned out across the bay for hours, and gradually the character of the wood emerged. There were soft spots under those cracks in the fiberglass and some damaged places from scrapes on a beach, but what was more apparent was the integrity of the wood. Its life seemed to extend beyond itself, beyond the living days of its source tree into an indefinite future. The fiberglass and epoxy and paint that protected it from natural decay were preserving an innate strength that began back where it was rooted and grew, its trunk upright, its form branching out to define a skyline, shade a hillside. The tree's wood had been cut by an axeman, cut again by a mill worker, cut again and shaped by the craftsmen at Lowell's. Dorik and I cared for that wood now, trimming and sanding away its weakened fibers to prolong its tenacity and endurance. We warmed it for days with heat lamps, shifting them morning and night to even out the drying. When it seemed that most of the dampness had gone we began covering up the wood again, sealing it away, shifting our attention from wood grain and fiber to the hull itself, to the function and structure of the boat. Many layers later—of putty, epoxy, extra fiberglass, more epoxy, primer and primer and paint and paint—our friends came and helped us carry our refurbished dory back to the water. I climbed in and rowed it back out to its mooring buoy. The boat and I were both riding high.

The two-hundred-year lineage of Lowell's craftsmanship stayed with me as a kind of conscience during those weeks of work on the boat. As I tied it up to its mooring in this sheltered Pacific Ocean cove, I thought of its birthplace on the other side of the continent. I have never been to the northeast corner of Massachusetts, where Simeon Lowell plied his craft on the Merrimack, just upriver from its emptying into the Atlantic. I try to imagine that shoreline—the riverbank, its trees and grasses and gravels, the intertidal waters where river and ocean meet, the eastward sweep out across the Atlantic. I think of it as a landscape more worn and aged than the precipitous and forested rise of the Alexander Archipelago islands along this North Pacific shore. But that's the dory's heritage, an easterly one. Community names around Amesbury reflect that inclination—Gloucester, Portsmouth, Exeter, Manchester, Derry, Newburyport, Hampton—influences of the English motherland so clearly repudiated during Simeon Lowell's lifetime. The little boat's new mooring juxtaposes its lineage against a mix of others. Place names around Sitka reflect the western colonization going on while the fledgling Lowell Boat Shop was supplying dories to fishermen on the eastern shore. Baranof, Chichagof, Kruzof, Partofshikov, Verstovia, Medvijie, Starrigavan, Aleutkina— the Russians claiming places in Sitka Sound, exploring the area in their eighteenth-century ships. The sixty years of their occupation accounts for the predominance of those robust place names rather than the softer guttural clicking words the indigenous Tlingit Indians used to describe places they knew long before the Russians arrived. Most of those original names have not been restored, although it was the Tlingit who stayed and the Russians who went home after the sale of Alaska to the United States in 1867. It is the present day Tlingit—20 to 30 percent of Sitka's population—that carry forward the much older heritage of human inhabitation here.

By necessity, the story of that inhabitation includes boats of one kind or another. The oldest stories tell of people arriving on Baranof Island's Sitka shores by canoe—the Tlingit Kiksadi clan from the south, the Kagwantaan and Coho clans from the north. They used their boats to gather food, to fish, hunt seal, travel to summer camps where they readied provisions for winter. A later style of those long carved wooden boats was the striking head canoe, its high prow squared off on top and painted on both sides with the bold forms featured in the art of Native people all along the northwest coast. Other boats appeared along Sitka's shores in the eighteenth and nineteenth centuries. By the early 1900s, there were photographs to document the influences that came with European and American settlement. Lovely lapstrake rowing skiffs floated at anchor or were pulled up on the beach. Sailing vessels were moored offshore and steamers traveling up from Seattle made Sitka a port of call. Not much later, fishing boats began to arrive and have stayed on to dominate the local waterfront. In late twentieth-century summer months, seven- and eight-hundred-foot luxury cruise liners steam into the sheltered water of Sitka Sound to drop anchor for a few hours and put their thousand passengers ashore. All around those floating city-ships, human-scale skiffs and trollers and cabin cruisers go about the business of daily life on the ocean's edge.

These histories of craftsmanship and place and maritime tradition all come to me through the dory. My boat often generates comments when we venture out; dories are not common craft in this part of the world. But serious mariners almost immediately acknowledge the place these boats have had in the human legacy with the sea. Adrift in Eastern Channel or exploring a cove I've not visited before or making my way from Thimbleberry Bay along the shore into town, I remind myself that these mountains and points and islands have been guiding people for thousands of years. The land gives shape to these waters at the ocean's edge. It changes vastness into defined space, named straits and bays and inlets that map the course of human passage. I go where others have gone, though my experience is particular—the lonesome warble of a loon in this spot, the first catch of a salmon in that, the deer bones resting on a grassy ledge above the water. With each trip, this place where I live expands to become more specific. And the dory affords me this growing intimacy, riding reliably over the water, its planks tight, its hull secure, its bow rising to whatever wave it meets. Each trip I entrust myself to its safekeeping.

In the Long Silence After, the Earth Still Breathes

On a moonlit fall night I stood out on our deck and listened. A looming silence was enveloped by soft lapping of water on the rocks below, a silence particular and empty. Just the day before, three young Sitka men had ventured out on a weekend hunting trip, enticed by the call for good weather and reports of the abundance of deer. Only one of them came home. From news reports I imagined a version of the story.

They had camped for the evening at the head of Silver Bay in a forest clearing just up from the beach. The day's adventure had heightened their spirits and the evening seemed just right—a camp supper, a few beers, shared jokes and banter by the fire, the night quiet around them, the water just beyond moonwhite and still. But their energies weren't quite spent. Two of them decided to take the skiff out for a short spin before turning in. The bay's glassy calm was hard to resist. Or perhaps they wanted to get a better view of the night sky. They pushed the boat offshore and in a minute the outboard roared to life. It settled into a steady drone, its pitch rising as the skiff picked up speed. Before long a white wake was flying out behind the boat as it whisked across the dark water. The two men looped and circled around the bay, exhilarated by the chill air and the black sky alive with stars. The moon shone on their faces and cast their shadows in the boat beside them. The night and the water were theirs. When it felt like time to head back to camp, the one in the stern pushed the tiller hard over to turn the boat around, but his motion was too sudden and too extreme. The skiff lunged up on its side and then flipped over in a fall that turned the whole night upside down. The water was suddenly too deep and and it quickly became too cold. Life's fullness that only moments before had thrilled them began to slip away.

On shore, their companion heard the engine quit abruptly and waited to hear it start again. He paced the shore, waiting, while the truth of the silence swelled to an echoing cry that came uncontrollably from his throat. He tossed in his sleeping bag, waiting, holding his hands over his ears to shut out the ringing quiet and then holding himself for the reassurance of his own live flesh and bone. He watched the morning come, waiting for help and for the shock to find its way to family and friends. He wept all the way home in the rescue boat, waiting for the hard knot in his chest to ease.

In the community the next day the ache spread itself

even to those who didn't know the two men lost. Imagined reruns began in many minds: if only he . . . if only they . . . if only it was all different. Instead, a bright sun refused the possibility of denial and people's days were broken again and again by moments of unsettling acquiescence. For those close, an agony of disbelief raged through them. For others an unspoken sorrow tinged their actions and words. For still others the sadness and emptiness were all too familiar. Sitka's watered boundary is a border on uncertainty. People here court the ocean and its inner waters, read its moods, test themselves against it, stand by to watch it roil in its own wildness. Its lessons go with the territory. The water's cold is more than most anyone can bear.

In front of our house that night, Thimbleberry Bay was bathed in white light. A whisper of air moving over the water turned it into a jeweled surface. The cedars beside the porch flickered and teased the darkness. The rippling murmur of a moving tide washed the rocks below. Across Eastern Channel the silhouetted hills framed both water and sky. There was room in that beauty for unbearable pain, I thought. Room for life and its passing, room for unspeakable private grief. Here was a moon-blessed benediction that would let us all go on.

When you wake to the morning of loss
nothing holds. Your empty world is undefined.
You must learn to breathe the too light air,

place your feet again, one at a time.
Find color in the flash that blinded you,
feel your way to rock and tree.
You must come to know proximity,
let the hills be themselves,
the waters cold, strong and deep.
Let days rise singly with the sun.
You must learn again to give thanks,
feel the strength of bone as you stand
clean in the nakedness of your grief.

A beach in a favorite local park offers a remarkable view
of the basin of mountains and water that hold the town
of Sitka. I stood there on a late afternoon one January,
watching the winter light fade to gray overhead and deep
blue behind me while a fiery golden gleam blazed out
from under a heap of clouds piled on the western horizon.
Sitka Sound was quiet. An easy wash of shallow waves
crisscrossed over the pebbly shore at my feet. Above that
cadenced wet rustling I heard the distant drone of a small
plane and found its flickering light moving low over the
water on its way home. A search plane, maybe. The troller
Camelot was missing. A break in a week of bad weather
had only recently afforded this calm.

On board the forty-eight-foot boat were a crew of two
and a golden retriever. They were out, perhaps, after a run
of winter kings. Whatever their catch of fish, they found
themselves caught by the grip of a storm that turned the
ocean into a flailing desperate nightmare. Looking out

across the present calm, it was hard to fathom the possibility of twenty- and thirty-foot seas, surging tons of water that mounted skyward until they crashed back on themselves, swollen roiling waves that shattered themselves against the rocks and outer shores of these islands. Such turbulence cleans out everything in its path, leaving only shards and pieces. It had left nothing of the *Camelot*. The search so far had been useless. Still people waited and hoped and prayed, but found little comfort in the recent calm. Its vast stillness only deepened the profound emptiness remaining, the space that, in the refusal that precedes grief, would be filled again and again.

I watched the search plane disappear from sight and slowly allowed myself to acknowledge my footing on solid ground. Just in front of me the water continued to laze its way toward shore over the flat shelf that extended the shallows and then dropped abruptly into a deep cut not far beyond. A littler farther out was the cluster of low forested islands that separate Eastern and Middle Channels—Galankin, Katz, Kutkan, Morne, The Twins—dark shaggy humps breaking the water. Out in Eastern Channel a flashing light marked the channel junction and the Rocky Patch: six red flashes, a pause, six more, a pause, six more. On the southern Twin, a green light flashed once every four seconds. I imagined these lights to be like stars, charting the way in the darkness, outlining the hundreds of miles of fractured land stretching along this coast. Much of it rises sharply, like the Pyramids beyond Eastern Channel, to three thousand feet or more, steep forested slopes black in evening light, summits capped white with snow. My eyes climbed to those high crests and moved from one to the next—the Pyramids joining Eureka and Lucky Chance to the east, which joined Bear, Verstovia, and the Sisters to the north. The crown of familiar peaks caught the trailing edge of evening light. They had been witness, I reminded myself, to every human story that had unfolded here.

I thought again about the shortened lives aboard the *Camelot*. In the anguish of loss it is not easy to come to terms with the land's duration, knowing that we must one day give ourselves to the earth. I wondered then if human sorrow isn't as old as these mountains, extending itself as it does beyond our bounds. The ache we feel is perhaps an earthly bond, grounding itself in flesh and bone. If so, nature's endurance must also embody our lessons for survival and healing, for in the long silence after death, the earth still breathes. That evening its comfort was a continuum of color—paling yellows and golds, hints of green deepening to blue that would become the darkness soon to be marked with stars. Tomorrow, another day of light and the persistence of green out of season. Or perhaps the sheltering boughs of trees in a winter rain. The return of herring and sea lion and whale out my window, the glide of gull and eagle. Maybe a fire's warmth or the flutter of chickadees at a feeder. The smoothness of river stones in my hand or the whisper of air through cedars. The ability to move, the ground underfoot, the impulse to go back out into the world.

The Edge of a Storm

When I went to the window in the morning and pulled back the stiff motel curtains, I looked through sheets of flying rain. But there was the ocean I had come for, visible over the top of a shrubby rise that fell away to edge the North American continent. The water was a furied reach that day, all the way from horizon to shore. Dark swells flailed under a deceptively flat sky, cresting and breaking chaotically, off in the distance and closer and closer to shore. Gusty winds topped the waves with arcs of spray that blew back at the gray bank of the storm. I watched and watched, savoring that first view, that initial moment of recognition, reacquainting myself as I would with an old friend I hadn't seen in some time. The familiar shapes and movements were there, the rise and rise and rise of a swell, the wave peaking skyward then starting to lean toward shore, the crest curling forward in a smooth arc of water, the arc tightening . . . tightening . . . then tumbling in a spill of white surf down the sloping face of the wave, the frothing water coming in and in and in. I tuned my ear to the ambient roar and watched some more, trying to settle with the ocean's mood that day. The roiling swells crowded each other, tormented by the fitful wind. To the north, they beat against rocky island pinnacles just offshore. To the south they raced at a tall headland, collided against its flanks, and exploded in spray and mist up its open face. I watched and watched, reconnoitering with the deep-rooted impulse that had brought me here.

We had arrived the night before, winding our way along the darkened Olympic Peninsula, peering through rain-streaked windows to find the road and the Ocean Park Resort at La Push. "Have you been here before?" the motel clerk had asked when we called to make a reservation. We hadn't. No televisions, no telephones, she went on, with the voice of a strict summer camp supervisor describing unacceptable activities. The only unit available has a kitchen, but the stove doesn't have an oven. Our room would be left open for us. We could register in the morning.

We parked in one of the last available spaces, suited up against the persistent squalls, and ferried our bags and food inside. The door from the parking lot opened into a small crowded bedroom. Beyond it was a more open kitchen and sitting area with windows on the ocean. It was definitely a unit for two. A double bed, two vinyl-covered straight-backed chairs at a small table, two cups, two glasses, two plates, two sets of silverware, a couch with room for two. Well-worn carpet covered the floor and dark wood paneling the walls, bare of any art. The essentials and nothing more, but it was warm and dry. We opened a bottle of wine and settled in. A noisy heater fan for the rooms above shut out the sounds of wind and rain. It cycled off in time for us to try to sleep while our upstairs neighbors entertained friends with beers and stories and laughs. The fan was still off when I woke in the middle of the night. Remembering where I was, I listened past the weather for the ocean's steady distant roaring and let it lull me back to sleep.

"Where would you like to go?" Dorik had asked when we were talking about this short November vacation. "The ocean," I said, without even thinking. Oceans pull on me like a homing instinct. The day I was born I interrupted a planned trip to the warm beach we frequented the years my family lived in Vengurla. Before long, I was a regular on those seashore visits. First a diapered newcomer on a beach towel; then a toddler with small hands holding fast to adult ones, my pudgy feet in the foamy remnants of broken waves; then a youngster floating over my-sized swells, diving under them, riding them to shore on a small wooden surf board. When their churning rumble pummeled me into the sandy undertow and filled my nose and mouth with water, I got up gasping and went out to do it again. The wet salt smell, the rhythm of approaching swells, the cadences in the constant thunder, the tumbling froth of water leading waves to shore, their eager race up the sandy beach and their yielding retreat—all these patterns rooted themselves for a lifelong hold.

Our motel window looked out on the Pacific Ocean just thirty miles south of its open run through the Strait of Juan de Fuca into Puget Sound. The continental edge that bounds it there begins at Cape Flattery and continues down to Cabo San Lucas at the tip of Baja California, broken only by rivers and occasional bays. North of Juan de Fuca all the way to Alaska that edge is fronted by myriad islands that break up the force of the Pacific's third-of-the-globe stretch before it reaches the North American landmass. But from our motel window there were a few isolated pinnacles and nothing more. Just that enormous basin of water, pulled by the moon, swept along by currents and storms, rolling ashore. It was not warm, either. No wonder it's intimidating, I thought, as I continued to watch from the dry vantage point of our room. We had ventured out toward the beach after we checked in, but five minutes of the blowing squall drenched us. So we changed out of wet clothes and resumed our positions: Dorik relaxed on the couch with a book; I stood at the window.

It wasn't until our check-in visit to the office that we realized the resort was run by the local Native American tribe, the Quileute. A couple of walls featured contemporary Indian crafts—tightly woven baskets of grass or bark, carved wooden miniature totems or plaques of mythical figures, white- or brown-skinned dolls in semblances of traditional dress. One of the clerks behind the counter had the strong features of her people—black hair, cedar skin, clear cheekbones. While she silently finished up our paperwork, I twirled the postcard rack. A couple of cards snagged more than my passing glance. One was an aerial photograph of La Push—the shoreline, the community, a boat harbor, and the island pinnacles close to shore. Two thin lines showed up in the water, running from the mainland out to those pinnacles. I puzzled a bit and then realized they were breakwaters creating a channel for boats leaving and entering the harbor. The ocean's mood that day made it clear why they were necessary.

The other postcard was a realistic painting of a traditional Indian canoe with six or eight men aboard. The canoe was angled down the front of a cresting wave. Another was breaking behind it. Other waves out in front were already reduced to white tumbling surf. The men in the canoe were eager. Their determination to ride out this roiling sea showed in their faces. Their well-muscled arms guided and worked their paddles through the water. I don't recall that there was any land in sight.

I left both postcards behind. When we went back to our room, I noticed a carved Thunderbird hung high on the front of our two-story motel building.

While Dorik absorbed himself in his book I kept watching the storm, roaming to the high sky and back, from horizon to shore, from the north pinnacles to the southern headland. The steady repetition of breaking waves mesmerized me for long minutes until some flinch of mind or nuance in the scene prodded my attention. A nuance like the bright light I thought I was seeing on the dark gray horizon. When I was certain, I said, "There's a boat out there." That simple reality made the ocean come alive with danger.

Dorik joined me at the window and we watched the light for some time before we were sure it was moving toward us over the faltering horizon. The bright spot slowly got bigger and we could see then that it was swaying from side to side, bowing toward the water first one way and then the other. There was no shape beneath it, only the bright arcing light making its way through the tattered seas. As it swung back and forth I could almost feel the boat rolling under my feet, the tight grip of my hands on a rail, the queasy lump in my stomach. At one point the light's arc widened—too far, it seemed—as the boat heeled over further in the heaving swells. My imaginary ride became a palpable knot of fear. Would it right itself? Was it taking water over the gunwales? Did the skipper have enough control? Finally a form emerged out of the gray and gradually defined itself as a fishing boat, bright spotlights atop its mast. I wondered how many people were aboard, how long they'd been out, how far they had ventured, whether they'd had ample warning of this storm. The closer it got, the better we could see the full extent of the boat's pitch and roll, and the more grateful I was to have my feet on solid ground. The skipper was guiding it toward the island pinnacles where the surge was crashing up the rock walls and swells were breaking and tumbling to shore. Trust him, I told myself in my nervousness. I remembered the aerial photograph, the breakwater. He knows where he's going.

At last the boat was in the lee of those towering rocks. We could see her seiner profile now, her bow riding over a cresting wave, her stern taking the following breaking sea. Then, for an instant, she became that painted open canoe, a group of determined, well-seasoned men aboard, reading the seas, skillfully bringing her home. And in that moment, the seiner and her crew became sheltered by all the Quileute seafaring years that went along with this place, all the experience passed from one generation to the next. Not invincible, but wise—to the ocean, to the weather, to the limits and capabilities of their boats and themselves. My fear backed down into respect. I imagined Quileute women, their years of faith and waiting, the wailing emptiness they must have known from time to time when a boat didn't come home. I stood up on my toes to watch the seiner nose safely into the harbor.

In the late eighteenth century, when Westerners arrived on this coast, the aboriginal Quileute territory spread over some seven hundred fifty square miles. Its northern reach was defined by the Soleduck River watershed and tributaries, from headwaters to their convergence into a single mouth on the ocean at La Push. The Hoh River watershed served as a southern boundary, snaking inland some fifty miles to the slopes of Mount Olympus. Today the Quileutes at La Push live on a one square-mile reservation established by the executive order of President Grover Cleveland in 1889, the same year a fire destroyed all the homes there. They are hemmed in not only by the reservation boundaries, but by the narrow Pacific Coast area of Olympic National Park that protects much of the peninsula's shoreline. The rest of the larger territory they once used is now owned by private interests or the federal government, much of it within the Olympic National Forest or the larger main body of the park. The hemlock, spruce, and red cedar rain forest on their lands was prized by the Quileute as a source of food and materials for clothing and shelter. They gathered fruits and berries, hunted deer and elk, and used roots, bark, and grasses for clothing and baskets. Much of the forest is gone now, prized by later settlers for its timber. In its place are "tree plantations" managed like agricultural crops by regional timber companies. Some of the Quileute have worked in the woods for these companies, but many have stuck by their seaward traditions. Historically, they were whalers and fishers. The rivers in their territory and the bordering ocean were home to salmon, steelhead, halibut, trout, octopus, and other delectables. Orca and gray whales—others too—moved offshore. These days, the Quileute don't go whaling, but their subsistence fisheries have developed into commercial enterprises. They are still seafarers, like their ancestors. Their large canoes have been replaced by modern fishing boats, but their prows still cut through the rolling surf that comes ashore at La Push. Foul weather or fair, they continue to bring their boats home, witness the seiner just then safe at harbor. When a second one followed a short time later, I climbed up on a chair to better watch and marvel at its surging ride to shore.

After the storm broke—after we had watched the solid dark cloud crack open, after the few minutes it took the gales to clear the sky—we went out to explore the beach. We found a cluttered montage of pebbly rocks and driftwood—flat round granitic stones, gray and green and red, some with streaks of quartz. Logs and branches and twigs and shards, piled together in mats of seaweed. The high tide brought foamy waves up over a slope of dark sand. A passel of kids oblivious to the wintry wind raced up and down that edge of sand, the water at their heels or over their ankles and up to their knees. Patient parents listened to their shouts and excitement, huddling behind logs, dressed in ensembles of bright rain gear and hats and gloves. An older gentleman had found a nook in the lee of a log and sat on the rocks, holding his cane upright, looking out to sea. We meandered along, past him and past the children, stopping to look at odd rocks or to brace ourselves against the wind, picking our way among scatterings of wood and kelp and debris washed ashore. Before long we came to the cutbank of a creek that had gouged a channel deep enough to keep us from going further. On our way back we wondered about a lone stump, taller than either of us, that stood in the wash of the tide. Its spreading base reached out five feet in diameter and buried itself deep in the sand. Could it be rooted there, a remnant of a forest that once edged an altered shore? Had it been placed there by the whims of natural forces? Could someone have planted it there deliberately to fool people like us? We wondered and should have asked. Instead we counted the rings of a log that was being chunked up for firewood. One hundred, two, three hundred thirty years at least, a tree that was standing, still growing, when the Quileute world began to expand and shrink at the same time, to be changed forever.

According to a Quileute story, the first white people they encountered came ashore from a grounded ship just off their beach. The schooner *St. Nikolai* had set sail from my home town of Sitka, Alaska, in September 1808, under the auspices of the Russian American Company, and had met its fate a couple of months later. The Quileute account

of the shipwreck and ensuing events was recorded sometime around 1909 at the request of an elder who related
the story through a translator to a Bureau of Indian
Affairs field officer on scene at the time. The elder was
Ben Hobucket, and his family had kept the story alive.
They had more than a passing interest in it. One of the
ship's survivors, a captive woman, had lived with the
Hobuckets for a while until she and others were rescued
two years after their ship had foundered. The full story is
a fascinating one of skirmishes between the coast natives
and their stranded visitors, of loss of life, of endurance
and survival. One thing made clear is that the people who
came ashore from the St. Nikolai were not entirely welcome among the Quileute or their neighbors, the Hoh
and Makah Indians. Perhaps they had some inkling of
what this visit portended. Perhaps they, like other Native
American tribes, had vision stories foretelling the coming of strangers and the threats posed to their territory
and way of life. What the Quileute might have done had
they known that the tables of captivity would be turned
on them within the lifetimes of their children is not particularly useful speculation. What is useful is a recognition of their knowledge, of their history with this place.
That's what had started to work its way under my skin.

Dorik and I left the rocky beachfront and walked on
past our motel, past a row of tiny beach cottages that
edged scattered houses and trailer homes, through puddles
of rain toward the breakwater and the harbor. We came
out on an open stretch of flat ground edged by a sloping
hill on one side and the ocean on the other. I have an

imprecise memory of these things: a new school building up on the slope, bright-colored playground equipment, a pile of black plastic pipe for an improvement
project out on the point. What I remember more clearly
are the canoes.

Beside an apparently abandoned single-story house
were two canoes—long wooden boats, narrow and deep,
each carved out of a single log. One rested behind the
house, the other was in the open and half full of rainwater.
The carver who had finished it had textured it inside and
out with neat rows of adze marks that ran lengthwise
from bow to stern. The exterior was painted black with
two red stripes angled across its bow. Narrow carved
wooden slats that served as seats were fitted into rectangular wooden holders placed below the gunwales. Some
of the seats were missing, others rested at cockeyed an-
gles in the boat. Perhaps this canoe was serving as a model
for a third one just taking shape nearby. Half a red cedar
log had been partially hollowed out with a chain saw.
Parallel cuts across its width made it easier to gouge out
most of the inner wood. The surfaces would have to be
finished with smaller hand tools. But the whole project
looked like it had been abandoned. A sheet of plastic that
must have once protected the carving was strewn haphaz-
ardly over the log and the ground, some of it buried in
water that stood in carved-out sections of the canoe. The
companion half of that cedar tree lay heart-down nearby.
The log when whole had been a bit smaller than the one
on the beach whose rings we had counted, a tree maybe
two or three hundred years old when it was taken down.

I wanted to believe it had been carefully selected and cut for this canoe. I wanted to believe this carving project was passing on skills and history and traditional knowledge to a new generation. I wanted to think that when spring came, people would be out here again, putting the plastic sheeting aside, bailing the water out, wrapping their hands around their tools. I wanted to believe all those things.

We walked on out to the point where we could look over to the harbor, and I wondered which of the boats moored there were the seiners we had watched come in. Circling around, we followed the road back toward the motel, past the main part of the community. A couple of lamps were on in a tidy white house next to the road. Other houses and mobile homes were crowded beside and behind it. I remember thinking how separate the vacationing community was from the people who lived here, the visitors over by the beach, the residents next to the school and the working harbor. I imagined they welcomed our visitor dollars, but I wondered how much they welcomed our presence.

We woke late the next day in our dark little room and opened the curtains to bright sun, scattered billowy clouds, and a lively north wind—the kind of day that would let us enjoy what we'd come for. There were two other beaches south of town. We decided on Third Beach and drove down to the trail head. The brown Park Service sign said 1.3 miles. We ambled along a narrow road through scrappy alders choked with underbrush—an old timber harvest area, probably the old logging road.

After a while we found ourselves on a footpath, walking through taller conifers and a lush understory of ferns and salal. The farther we got from the highway, the bigger the trees were, and the more we sensed what the country and forest had been like in the years before Indian reservations and timber companies. The high canopy of filtered light. The sturdy pillars of old trees. The carpet of plants. Room for animals and people to move. The saturated deep green of a mature rain forest. I found it agonizing to think about how little of it remained.

As we walked along I kept waiting, anticipating the point when I could hear the breaking waves and smell the salt spray in the air. I wanted to be wrapped in that wash of sensation and pattern and movement. I wanted a refuge, however temporary, from an unsettling world. The steady roar came first, and then the earlier-than-I-remember familiarity of looking between the trees to the water beyond. As we followed the zigzagged trail down a steep high stream bank, the tangy salt fragrance rose to greet us. Then at last the finishing pieces—a crescent sand beach several miles long, a high edge of bleached driftwood, and the sunlit sea green water swelling and cresting, swelling and cresting, tumbling white, rolling to shore. I felt myself give way to a smile of delight.

A rising tide confined us to the few yards between the driftwood and the higher reaches of foamy water that raced up and down the beach. We walked north into a steady chill breeze. Here and there a stone or clamshell figured the sand. Here and there a tangle of kelp, a plastic bottle, a piece of rope, a fallen smaller tree from the bank above. We found a good log and sat huddled together to watch the ocean. The wind topped the waves in sprays of white light that Dorik said looked like the sunlit manes of wild running horses. Savoring his image from childhood against the backdrop of my own, I longed for the ease of that past. It wasn't here.

Clouds raced each other across the sky. Before too long a dark gray bank headed our way and urged us to amble back toward the trail. Dorik played a teasing tag game with the waves that swept over the sand, encouraging me to join him, but instead I watched the frothy lace of salty bubbles disappear into the sand. I wondered if Quileute canoes used to come ashore here.

By the time we got back to our motel room, another strong weather front had moved in. We let the darkness come and settled on the couch with our books, using one of the chairs as a coffee table for our small tumblers of wine. I read in fits and starts, wrestling with the sense that I didn't belong here. When I woke in the dark of early morning and realized the electricity was out, I pulled up the quilted bedspread and lay awake listening to a car or two going by on the road—perhaps the local repairmen called from sleep to fix the problem. If so, I was grateful to them. The wind and the ocean roared. I wondered what the Quileute knew of silence—perhaps only the deep silence of loss. At last the porch light outside our room came back on and I drifted into sleep.

In the morning we turned in our key and the extra plate we'd borrowed, got a brief "Okay" from the motel clerk, and headed down the road. A ways out of town we

passed a new housing development built for members
of the tribe and their families—blue box houses spread
along a driveway up into a clear-cut. I imagined the clean
new walls inside, the smell of fresh paint and new carpet,
the shiny appliances. A large stump stood as a sentry at
the entrance, other smaller ones landscaped the yards. A
wet snow was falling, covering the raw ground in a soft
blanket of white. We drove on by. Aching for comfort, I
closed my eyes. My memory found its way to these lines
by Philip Levine:

> But snow is nothing.
> It has no melody or form, it
> is as though the tears of all
> the lost souls rose to heaven
> and were finally heard and blessed
> with substance and the power of flight
> and given their choice chose then
> to return to earth, to lay their
> great pale cheek against the burning
> cheek of earth and say, There, there, child.

Thoughts on Trees:
Who Could Live Without This Grace?

Our Christmas tree came down one night in a Southeast Alaska storm. Dorik and I were curled together under our comforter, sleeping as best we could between house-trembling gusts of wind. Their menacing roar rose to frenzied pitches that sent broken twigs and branches clattering across the deck and roof. But when the tree fell, the ground shuddered. We felt the blow come up through the foundation of the house and it put us immediately on our feet. I realized, as we donned bathrobes, that I had been startled out of a dream in which I had heard the sharp crack before the fall. The sound rang clear now in my ears, as though a recording of the sequence was being played backward.

Out on the porch we grabbed at our robes to keep them wrapped around us. The slender beams of our flashlights caught snatches of the fury, cedar and hemlock boughs thrashing against the darkness in the roar of the wind. My hair mimicked those branches and flailed across my face. I went to one corner of the deck that surrounded the house, Dorik to the opposite, looking for the tree that had hit. We met each other back at the door, surprised and confused. Nothing. No trunk or limb on the porch. Nothing next to the house. Even the smaller branches and twigs had been blown somewhere else. Puzzled, we went back inside and had to force the door shut against the wind. The storm heckled us the rest of the night, pushing at the edges our skittish sleep. The hours before daylight stretched on and on in the roaring darkness.

Our puzzle was easily solved in the morning. Dorik went early into town, and I watched him start up the trail. Forty feet from the house he stopped, looked to either side, and stooped down to go underneath something. Then I saw the branches poking up unnaturally from the huckleberry bushes, and went out to see what had happened. The dark scaly trunk of a hemlock lay across the trail, the broken end tapering to a sharp point along the diagonal line of its fracture. After a minute or two we found the section of tree that had held ground. The side that faced us was intact and climbed thirty feet skyward before it came to a splintered stop. Its other side exposed a raw length of the tree's inner core. It had split vertically and twisted around in its fall, shaking the earth when it landed, its heart face up to the sky. Its profusion of short needles spread an unseasonal green through the huckleberry bushes; its branches reached for the air where they belonged.

The tree lay where it fell for a few days before we cut it up. Dorik trimmed off the limbs and tossed them down the bank to me. I gathered them back together into the random association of a pile, nothing at its center, nothing to connect the boughs to each other, an unwieldy heap of soft needles and twigs askew. He then cut the trunk into rounds that I carried, one at a time, to stack on the porch in a much more tidy arrangement, a pyramid of solid wood cylinders, nine or ten inches in diameter, butted up against the wall, an order completely at odds with the tree's natural form. The rounds were later rent apart by the heavy blows of a splitting maul and restacked to await their turn in a woodstove.

That hemlock was still on my mind when it came time to find a Christmas tree, and I went back out to that random pile of greens. To my surprise, most of the needles held firm to the boughs. Hemlock have a reputation for shedding needles quickly when they get dry. I pulled the top of the tree out from the pile and stood it up on the butt end of its tapered trunk. Its branches spread unevenly from the center, some short and full, others longer and more spare, making it flat on one side and bushy on the other. The slender twig at the very top curved down characteristically in a graceful nod. In Northwest Coast Indian legend this is the hemlock's humble acknowledgment of its second place to the cedar. That afternoon, it struck me as the tree's humbler acquiescence to its fall.

We cleared a place in the living room and brought the treetop inside. Without a stand to hold it upright, we leaned its flat side against a wall of windows and wrapped a colorful shawl around its base. Some of the boughs draped down and swept the floor. Everything in the room made way for the presence of the tree, a token of the green

complexity that gives life to this northern coast. Having
that green inside warmed us. Trimming it with strings
of light was a gesture of reciprocation. Adorning it with
decorations—ornaments made by hand, with particular
care—was a small human tribute to its sustaining form.
On its topmost slender branch, in the arc of that graceful
curve, we hung a delicate angel.

Around the corner from our house—the corner formed by
the point of land marking the beginning of Silver Bay—
lies the idle Alaska Pulp Corporation mill. It is tucked
away in its own little cove, out beyond Sitka's residential
areas, on a long arm of water that cuts back into Baranof
Island. After thirty years of operation, the mill recently
closed its doors and stopped converting trees to chemical-
grade pulp.

Whenever I approach the mill site—either by water or
by road—I try to prepare myself for the turn around that
certain bend when its whole industrial scape appears in
front of me. The sight is always jarring, even when I know
it's coming. When the mill was operating, my eye was
immediately drawn to the plumes rising from the stacks.
Then the scene in front of me filled itself out with the
buildings and docks, the big flat cylindrical tanks on the
hill, and the various other structures not recognized by
my layperson's eye. In front of the mill, a dirty foam in
the water was corralled by a floating containment boom.
Boats and tugs chugged around the docks and the bay. On

the opposite shore of the narrow inlet, raft after raft after raft of logs floated at the surface, secured by cables to the shore. Directly above where they were tethered and on along the extended bank of the inlet, a dark thick forest of hemlock and spruce spread over a steep hillside. That bank of trees still faces the mill site. The log rafts below them are gone now. The industrial plant across the bay is quiet, empty, useless.

I used to stand at our living-room window and watch tugs hauling those log rafts to the mill. From a distance, the rafts looked like they were made up of a single layer of logs all banded together, but in fact they were bundles of logs secured to each other. If one or two logs floated at the surface, another eight or ten were bundled to them under water. They floated side by side and end to end, strung together sometimes to the length of a football field. The tugs always looked like they were barely moving. Sometimes there were two—one out in front to pull, another alongside the raft to nudge it along. No doubt the bundles provided a good deal of resistance in the water, but the weight alone of all that wood must have been what strained those boats. The huge engines roiled the water in an impressive show of power. The logs crept along behind with hardly a sound. They would soon be tethered beneath that hillside thick with trees.

The irony of that picture was striking—hundreds and hundreds of dead trees floating below a hillside of the living. Still I couldn't quite make it real. By the time those logs were tied up there in front of the mill, they were no longer trees. Back in the clear-cut when they first crashed to the ground, when they were denuded of the limbs of green that breathed for them, they had already begun a transformation which would so completely alter them that, in the end, they could never be recognized as trees. They would be changed from sustainers of life, the lungs of the planet, to consumer goods that mask any possible resemblance to their original form—rayon dresses and skirts and blouses, for example, featured in endless fashion catalogs and department stores. Paging through those catalogs I try and try to make a connection between those elegant clothes and the forest that graces the Alaska Pulp Corporation's front yard, my front yard, the whole archipelago that makes up Southeast Alaska. I cannot make that connection. The transformation has been too severe. Those trees have been too completely consumed.

Harlan Hubbard was a man I would like to have known. He understood something about love that, if I ever understood it, I have lost. He was an anomaly in modern American life, living without most of the conveniences and comforts I depend on and take for granted. He and his wife spent years on a shanty boat, floating the rivers and the bayous of the South and Midwest. When they settled down, they built themselves a simple house and lived elegantly in the Kentucky woods for some forty years without electricity, hot running water, a telephone, or an indoor toilet. They ate mostly food from their garden, fish from the river, or small animals they could hunt. They bartered with friends more than they depended on the cash economy. They spent time each day reading — Shakespeare and Milton, Emerson and Emily Dickinson, Proust and Jung and Henry James. Together, they played the music of Bach and Schubert and Brahms and Beethoven on their violin and Steinway grand. Hubbard was an accomplished painter; he also avidly recorded musings and observations in his journals. And he enjoyed work — physical labor, using the muscle and bone of his body to keep himself tied to the land where he lived. He took as much pleasure in the day's work as he did in the time of rest that followed. He died in 1988, his wife Anna just two years before that.

The Hubbards lived a life I often imagine but cannot live. Many people went to meet Harlan and Anna, as though a longing for something they had not achieved in their own lives could be partially relieved by direct contact with someone who had. I doubt I would have been bold enough to make such a pilgrimage had I been close by, but I would have liked to have had Harlan help me understand what he seemed to know intuitively about love — that it is vital not only because it ties us to our own kind, but because it grounds us fundamentally in the world. What Harlan Hubbard understood that I am only now coming to realize is that without affection for that world — the one beyond the human, the continuum of living things of which we are only a part — we allow ourselves to forget what is actually there and to strip it of its essential nature.

Wendell Berry has written a short biography of Hubbard in which he comments,

> Harlan was uninterested in, and he mistrusted, thought apart from its objects and apart from affection for its objects. If modern civilization seemed confining to him, this is one of the reasons why. It reduces creatures to ideas and to money-values, which eventually exclude the creatures themselves from consideration. If one is going to destroy a creature, the job is made easier if the creature if first reduced to an idea and a price. Reduction, that is, facilitates manipulation or use without affection, and use without affection is abuse.

I live in a house made of wood, a house that sits nestled in a forest of hemlock, spruce, and yellow cedar. A single yellow cedar post rises two stories from the living-room floor to the ceiling, supporting the center beam of the house and the two beams that support the loft floor. Those beams and others are also yellow cedar, locally milled with rough surfaces. The evidence of these beams' life as trees is all over them—in their length and girth, the grain of the wood, the knots that show where their branches were. I imagine the builders, Jack and Margaret Calvin, picking the beam trees carefully as they cleared just enough space at the forest's edge for the house. The two cedars that nudge the deck stand like companions to the tall pole inside.

The pulp mill down the bay from us is testimony to an

altogether different use of trees. In order to do what that mill did to trees—transform them into chemical-grade pulp to manufacture products like rayon or graphite fibers for use in fly rods and military aircraft—one must put aside one's perceptions of the trees' original form and place in a forest. We have long been consumers of trees, using them to build our houses, burning their wood to keep ourselves warm, turning their fibers into paper and other products. We are well practiced at that shift from perceiver to consumer, from one walking in the forest to one imagining what could be done with all that wood. But when our uses of trees become as distant as rayon and aircraft are from a four-hundred-year-old spruce, we find it harder and harder to remember them in their natural context. The closer our use of trees stays to their original form, the easier it is for us to hold that spruce in mind as we use it—not the idea of wood transformed into some other substance, but the spruce itself, its wood and bark and needles, its height and girth and shade, its centuries of growth. Without this connection to the actual tree, we have little chance, in our uses of the forest, for the kind of affection Harlan Hubbard understood was necessary to live well in the world. In a 1937 journal entry, he wrote:

> The mind tries to live by the artificial structure of the world, but the body will have none of it, holding to primeval forces. People try to be all mind. . . . this has gone so far that now . . . the earth itself is but an idea. As animal[,] man has suffered from this and degenerated. . . . The only hope and consolation is the

perception of beauty, the revelation today of that which was God. It too has been crucified.

In the winter, we use a woodstove to heat our house. Most of the wood we burn comes to us by water. When the pulp mill was operating, we could depend on free-floaters that broke away from those many log rafts. Now we depend on high tides to dislodge drifters from random beaches. When we spot logs floating in the bay in front of our house, our firewood work begins. We gather rope, staples, and a hammer, pump up the eight-foot inflatable boat, and row out to claim our catch. The biggest log I have hauled in was close to three feet in diameter at the butt end and over fifty feet long. The image is a convoluted one—the remaindered trunk of a centuries-old spruce on its side in the water, tethered to a small air-filled boat, the tree's accumulated years of mass and weight being moved by the few muscles in my arms and back that pulled on the boat's oars. It was a slow journey to shore. As much as not, the inflatable was yanked around by the tons of wood in that log, but the boat and I had the slight advantage of a little control. The tide was high. I tethered that fallen Sitka spruce to one its size that stands on the beach fringe, close to the water.

With the ebb of the tide, we went down to see where the log was left to lie. It stretched across the beach parallel to the water line, grounded on a bed of sand and rocks. The work of cutting it up couldn't begin without a bit of maneuvering. We dug along both sides of the log for a stretch of a few yards and hollowed out enough space underneath it so the tip of the chain saw blade would miss the sand and rocks. I cleared those piles of beach away while Dorik started the saw. Its whining roar consumed all other sound. He sized the blade length against the log's diameter and came up short, so he started the cut from one side. The saw's whirling teeth ripped across the log, and spruce chips flew faster than I could see them. I watched the saw blade slowly inch its way down until it had almost come through to the beach sand. Then Dorik pulled the saw out, switched places, and met his cut from the other side. Several long minutes later, the cut round began to lean away from the log. Dorik worked the saw carefully through the last inch of wood, keeping the blade tip off the beach. Through the snarl of the saw, I heard that final outer layer of wood crack before the round thudded down on the sand.

While Dorik continued to work the chain saw, I rolled the round up the beach to begin splitting. When I laid it down, fresh cut up, I could see the grain and look for clues as to how it was likely to split. I checked for knots and placed the iron wedge between them, toward the outer edge on a line my eye said would cut directly across the tree's core. Tapping the wedge with the splitting maul, I set it firmly in the wood and then began to strike in earnest. The hard ping of metal on metal rang in my ears, vibrated up my arms, and echoed around the cove that protects our beach. The wood held solid. The wedge inched into it through the brute force of each of my strokes. Slowly a crack began to form, and with every blow it worked its way toward the center of the round. I could hear the wood giving way now, cracking and popping each time I brought the maul down. I swung again and again, again and again, until a final *pop!* The round came apart and the piercing metallic ring of that last stroke chased the wedge all the way down into the sand.

I pulled the halves apart and sat down on one of them to look at the other. It was beautiful wood, its heart with a pale golden red sheen and a grain as straight and true as Sitka spruce can be. It smelled damp and sweetly fermented, with a bitter tinge of sap. The long wood fibers felt smooth when I ran my fingers along them. The knots on the outside showed up in the center as tips where branches had started to grow horizontally. One was close to the newly split surface. A bulge showed where the main trunk had made way for it, the straight grain curving just enough to enclose the branch tightly. Each ring of the trunk, each year of the tree, wrapped itself around that branch as though holding it in place. That would be a stubborn spot for me—a place where the tree had so deliberately reinforced itself that it wouldn't come apart easily. I had learned to work around those places. My splitting maul had bounced right off them many times. My skill as a wood splitter was hardly matched to the design of the tree.

Still I eyed that half round for cues, hoisted it up on another block of wood, and began. First in quarters. The halves were big enough that I used the wedge again. The wood gave way more easily now that it was no longer a solid round. The quarters fell apart with just a few strokes. I set one up on the block, abandoned the wedge, and turned the maul in my hands to use its sharp edge. Imaginary pie-piece lines radiated out from the center and served as my guides. No knots in this quarter. I raised the maul. As I brought it down I let my hands slide along its handle to the end. *Ka-chunk.* The blade hit the outer rings of the wood and went all the way through to the block underneath. A tidy length of triangular wood fell to the beach. The motion was simple and clean. I repositioned the rest of that quarter and swung again. The piece split neatly in two. Three more swings to split each section crosswise, and I had stove-size pieces that landed on the beach with an almost hollow sound.

These knot-free quarters made the rhythm and motion of this physical work a pleasure—the heft of the maul in my hands, the flex of muscles in my back and arms, the precise placement of the stroke, the clean break where the wood comes apart. I was seduced by my own control over the tools and the wood. Each swing of the maul was a test of accuracy and judgment, and every section that broke up easily called for another. I paid more attention to my own satisfaction than I did to the diminishing reality of that spruce until I came up against a knot in the wood. Then the twisted, curving fibers resisted my strokes and what felt like a clean, swift motion turned into a contest of strength. I worked relentlessly, blow after blow, against these remnant branches that held tenaciously to their years of growth. My earlier

deftness with the maul came to feel like a clumsy bru-
tality. Eventually I got most of the knobby pieces trimmed
down to stove size. Particularly stubborn ones I left for
Dorik to cut up with the saw. My pile had gotten big
enough to haul up the hill and stack in the woodshed. I
laid down the maul. Piece by piece, I carried the broken
tree in my arms.

I am a practiced user of trees. I am a reader and writer
dependent on books whose paper comes from the forest.
I eat at a wooden table, sleep on a wooden bed, find shelter within walls and a ceiling of wood. Each step I take
across our wooden floor is dependent on the inherent
strength of trees. I would like to be able to acknowledge
the trees that are enfolded in a number of things I use
and enjoy, but in many cases, it is easy to overlook their
presence. I forget that the film in my camera is made of
celluloid, a by-product of trees. The music I enjoy is
played on a variety of wooden instruments, but I rarely
take account of the tree whose wood allows such resonance. A favorite Eskimo-style mask that hangs on one of
our walls is carved out of alder. I don't often think about
where the tree might have grown and who cut it down.
Another wall in our house displays a thirty-year-old set
of Breughel reproductions from Holland, printed on fine
paper. It is hard to imagine the trees whose lives are forgotten in those smooth thin sheets colored now with
landscapes and human forms.

Perhaps it is my workplace that forces me to acknowledge my presumptions as a consumer. The office is crowded with the remnants of trees—magazines, computer manuals, books, manila folders, scotch tape, newspapers, tablets, telephone books, Post-it notes, calendars, stationery, mailing labels, six file drawers full of records on paper and another four drawerfuls in cardboard boxes. Correspondence stacks paper on one side of my desk, bills to be paid on another. Wastebaskets fill quickly with drafts of projects, junk mail, used envelopes, and old notes to myself. I take it all for granted in the business of getting work done. It is its own forest, which I rarely see. There are too many intervening stages between those trees and me.

But when I stoke our woodstove in winter, I can look over the knots and grain in each piece of wood. I can recall the feeling of the maul in my hands, the rounds of wood I rolled up the beach, the chips flying from the chain saw. I can remember the log when it was whole and imagine fairly easily the hillside where it might have grown as a tree, a scarred slope now, a clearing of stumps and slash where shoots of the green low-growth are preceding the next generation of spruce. But in my mind I can see the tree, its years towering skyward, its bough tips brilliant green with new growth, its scaly gray trunk spreading out into the ground. On chilly days, I open the stove and put wood on the fire, then sit low on the hearth and soak up that spruce heat in my back.

When you fly down the coast from Sitka to Seattle on a clear day, you can't help but be struck by that ragged edge of the continent and the seemingly endless swath of mountains that stubble the earth's surface there not far from the ocean's edge. The coastline looks like it has been deliberately shredded—long jagged fingers of land reach out into the ocean as though they were grasping at something not there. The mountain range immediately behind crests with summit after sharp summit of snow. Intermittently, big snowfields have enough spread to give way to glaciers that snake between the peaks down to a lake or river or saltwater inlet. The flanks of these mountains and the valleys and lowlands are dark with a carpet of forest. You don't have to look for long before you begin to see shaved patches—rectangular brown blocks on a slope here, in a valley there, or along an extended flank of hillside. Thin lines quickly become apparent, winding over the land, perhaps from one patch to another or down to the water's edge in a bay or inlet. You might even make out a clearing there, and another rectangle floating in the water. From the air, these shaved patches look almost like fields on a farm. Their edges are tidy and they spread over the landscape like a quilt of planted crops on fertile soil. The farther you go, the more of them you see. These are harvest units in the temperate rain forest that stretches along the Alaska and British Columbia coasts. They are connected to the world of economics and industry by logging roads carved out for trucks to haul limbed trees from the clear-cuts to the water where they get rafted together and towed to a pulp or sawmill.

I find it much easier to look at clear-cuts from the air than from their edge along a highway or river valley or passage of water. From a plane I am struck by how widespread they are; I can think of the cuts as scars. But in a plane I am not face to face with the gaping wounds I witness on the ground—a scattered congregation of stumps, shards of broken limbs, the earth scoured raw where the trees were dragged out of the cut. I wrestle mentally with the various arguments for and against clear-cut logging, but none of them relieves the knotted ache that grows in me as I face one of these harvest units. I try to think of the regeneration of trees, of the ones that may grow back here in fifty, one hundred, two hundred years, but I can't get past the fact that this forest has been forever altered. I try to think of all the wood products I use as some justification for this mutilation, but I can't quell my uneasiness. My eyes can hardly stand the sight of this broken piece of land.

I recently attended a meeting—one of many of its kind—with a team of Forest Service planners who are working on a design for future management of the Tongass National Forest. I sat and listened to testimony from a group of concerned citizens, all of whom love this place where they live and were eager to see substantial changes in the existing timber cutting plans. They all spoke from the heart. One woman had written down her thoughts for someone else to read because she knew she wouldn't be able to get through them without breaking down. She admitted this to the planners there, and one of them responded with some sympathy, but said he believed the best policy was to lead with the mind and follow with the heart.

I listened with a deepening sadness and found my mind returning again and again to an image of a sculpture I had once seen of a life-size female torso carved in marble. The sculptress had used the stone to its best advantage. The grain was highlighted in the curves of the shoulders and breasts, in the sweep of the hip, in the gentle arc of the lower back and spine. The upper back of the torso was painted in a confusion of black brush strokes—random, uneven, violent. On the front, a sharp triangle had been cut away over the heart—between the breasts and extending down to the navel. It too was painted black. The sculpture was titled *Clear-Cut*.

I went away from the meeting that day thinking about love. I wondered how far, as a society, our minds might take us before we would no longer know how to let our hearts be taken by a forest. I wondered if, even now, we would be able to find our way there. I found myself haunted and perturbed by the recollection of Harlan Hubbard's words: "The only hope and consolation is the perception of beauty, the revelation today of that which was God. It too has been crucified."

The hill behind our house is covered with trees. Yellow cedar and hemlock predominate, but here and there are Sitka spruce. The trees serve as a quarter-mile buffer between the house and the road. Every day I walk through them along a trail that uses their roots to define itself. Some are steps that support my weight going up or down, others carve out a space for my foot to fall. I move through the trees some days almost oblivious to their presence. They allow me that self-centeredness. Other days I run my hand down their trunks, comforted by their tenure and the shelter they provide. They allow me that indulgence too. Sometimes I stop to look at the sky through the high canopy of their branches. In a storm that canopy becomes a sea of swaying trunks and thrashing boughs. In a heavy rain, water runs down the trunks and drips constantly from the boughs to the forest floor. On a bright morning, the sun streaks through them to dazzle the green under-story of huckleberry and menziesia. At evening, low light turns graying cedar bark to a rich red brown. Life comes full cycle in this forest. Dead trees have fallen and nurtured new growth. Some still stand tall among the living. A few of those have been recently cut, but the base of their lives firmly holds the ground. New seedlings are taking root around them wherever there is room.

This stand of forest is likely to remain as long as this piece of land stays in the ownership of people who care about the trees. I do not hold title to these acres and my own tenure here will certainly be shorter than that of the trees. But my mind and heart have moved through them daily for the span of a decade and more. They have settled me. They have helped my spirit take hold.

This seven-acre stand is both refuge and home, the place from which I venture out into the world. I pull this forest around me when I listen to foresters and policy makers describe their plans for timber sales and the harvest of trees. These hemlock and cedar and spruce stand as reminders behind all the paper and books and wood that I use. In the next raging winter storm, I will huddle in a safe corner of the house to watch the fury, and dread the wrenching crack before a fall. With the storm's passing I will marvel at the stillness and resilience and steadfastness of these trees. They are teaching me what Harlan Hubbard understood:

> Man's life on this earth—who has courage to face it? Yet there are the trees, against the dark sky, black bare trees, springing from the earth to flower, swaying in the wind, the low hollow moan of the wind. Who could live without this grace?

The Right Place for Love

Earth's the right place for love:
I don't know where it's likely to go better.

—Robert Frost

Today I watched a varied thrush die. Our porch was
alive with birds—juncos, sparrows, and thrushes—
chittering and skittering around the feeders I had been
filling daily during the unusual two-week snow. Dorik
and I were sitting at the dining-room table, watching
with delight. The smaller juncos dominated the feeder
perches while the sparrows and thrushes scuffled about
below. Suddenly, in a whirring instant of alarm, they all
took flight. One thrush tried to veer off into the open
stretch alongside the house, but was foiled by the sudden shape glass gives to air. He smashed into the window, hard, two or three feet from where I sat. I gasped
and threw my hands up in front of my face as though my
own life were in danger. Then there was the silence after

and the wrenching moment of uncertainty. Dorik stood
up to look.

"Is he down?" I asked.

He nodded, but added, "He might be all right."

I hesitated a few seconds and then headed for the door.
Outside, the bird congregation had already returned. They
completely ignored the wounded thrush who lay on his
back, mustard yellow feet clutching the empty air. I approached slowly. Soon I could see that his eyes were still
bright, his orange breast pulsing with rapid breaths. He
opened and closed his beak haltingly. I spoke softly, apol-
ogizing, my uncertain steps all too loud in the crystallizing
snow. Crouching down, I reached my hand out carefully,
not wanting to startle him, but found that I was the one
who flinched, so foreign was that soft form to my touch,
so precarious its moment. I stood again, shook my hands
in anguish, and almost walked away. With all those signs
of life maybe he would be all right. But he lay in cold
snow. Surely I should move him from there. I shifted
cautiously to a position where I could use both my hands
to pick him up. What if I would need to end his life in
mercy? My heart turned. But I crouched down again,
and at last pushed my trembling hands gently under him
through the snow to cup his warmth in my palms. When
his head fell limply against my fingers I knew my efforts
were in vain. Still, I asked Dorik to bring a box and a
couple of towels. I nestled him there to rest. His life filled
only a few more minutes. Then his breathing stopped.
The brightness in his eyes was gone. When I went out a

bit later that morning, I took his still-warm body up the trail and found a hollow under a tree that became his grave.

I harbored that thrush's death much of the rest of the day and wondered about my timidness as I tried to help. The tender fear that filled me seemed like another side of love, a connection I couldn't make into anything more than sentimentality until I thought about it in the context of a startling piece of scientific information I'd learned some months earlier. It came from poet and biologist Melinda Mueller in a talk she gave about myth and theory, about creationism and evolution. Her talk incorporated a wonderful review lesson about DNA that I'd been mulling over ever since. Because she is skilled in both poetry and science, she laid out her review in the metaphor of language, and that helped fix it in my mind.

The DNA alphabet, she reminded us, is made up of four letters, one for each of the nucleotides—adenine, guanine, cytosine, and thymine—that pair themselves across the double spiral of the DNA molecule. That alphabet arranges itself along the DNA strand in three-letter sequences or words. With a four-letter alphabet, there are sixty-four possible three-letter words. Each DNA cell contains billions of these nucleotide pairs, sequencing themselves in three-letter words that are arranged in any number of ways, creating the possibility of an infinite number of stories. Each of these stories is distinct, and corresponds to a particular species of plant or animal, giving us the biological diversity we know to be the gamut of life on this planet. But the sixty-four words in the DNA cells of all of those species—plant and animal alike—are precisely the same sixty-four words. And in every species, those words mean precisely the same thing. All living things on earth are linked by a common language.

I thought about that thrush against the backdrop of this biological and earthly bond of a common chemical language contained in our separate DNA cells. His story and mine were clearly different, of course. The particular sequence of his sixty-four words laid out the genetic code that made him a bird, that determined his size and the shape of his beak. Its certain order spelled out the details that created the sharp necklace stripe of black feathers around his orange neck. It determined that he would prefer the coniferous forest habitat outside my windows, that he would be attracted to the sunflower seeds I offered. That distinct genetic code gave him the trilling voice of an early singer of spring. My own DNA contained a parallel story that laid out an analogous set of characteristics— human being, female, fair skin, dark eyes, medium build, soft voice, the perceptive faculties to pay attention to birds. But behind all those species-specific details, in the genetic subworld that distinguished us, bird from human, the words that were strung together to create our definitive stories were sixty-four consistent words whose meanings stayed true across the species.

I remember being astonished by this gem of scientific

knowledge when Melinda laid it out. I was also embarrassed by my astonishment. Surely such rudimentary information was common knowledge. Why had I missed out? A bit of historical retrospective reminded me that, although the structure of the DNA molecule had been discovered in 1953, the full genetic code and its universal application across all species wasn't understood until the late 1960s—too late to filter into the high-school biology class that was the last focused dose of science I'd received. That eased some of my embarrassment, but the astonishment still remained. Why, I wondered, didn't more people pay attention to this bit of biological bedrock? Why hadn't it revolutionized the way we thought of ourselves, the way we lived our lives?

Dorik remembers being in Washington, D.C., the day that President Lyndon Johnson held a news conference at the Smithsonian to announce an extraordinary breakthrough with DNA. Though the memory isn't altogether clear, Johnson's announcement most likely was about the fact that scientists had cracked the full genetic code. The presidential delivery must have been intended to underscore the importance of this scientific news. But even Dorik, with his curious and attentive mind, when offered the rare opportunity to hear the word firsthand, opted to read about it the next day. I probably had the option of watching the news on television, but my high-school interests were otherwise. I wonder now if my biology teacher took it in. She, at least, would have understood its significance. My perspective was more likely to be akin to that of many other people—untrained in the complexities, unlikely to be mindful of the shifting parameters of science unless they directly affected my personal life. What I often fail to realize is the extent to which they can and do. And in many respects, the more we know by way of science, the broader the context for our lives and the more uncertain we are of our own importance. It is no wonder many of us, almost by default, leave the world of scientific discovery alone.

But thirty years later, the news about DNA struck home. I was fascinated by the paradox within it—the core that unifies all living species and the simultaneous possibilities for infinite diversity. I imagine that the diversity piece of the paradox was celebrated as the miracle of the discovery. Clearly, the extraordinary DNA structure, its distinctions, species by species, and its replication process, cell by cell, was ingenious almost beyond belief. And that part of the miracle reaffirmed our human uniquenesses, underscoring the way history has helped us come to think of ourselves—as a singular species of distinct individuals, each with our own remarkable selection of traits, set apart and above other animals by our capabilities, and certainly from plants by our physical characteristics. But the other piece of the DNA paradox was what astonished me. The miracle was the common language, the steadfast bond, the necessary connection, the irrevocable relationship, the divine intersection, the underlying coherence, the unquestionable consistency.

Perhaps my tenderness toward that thrush was mere sentimentality, but, then again, perhaps the emotion was grounded in this scientific and holy truth. And perhaps my timidness and uneasiness as I tried to help that bird lay in the fact that, almost all of my life, I had been unaware of this truth, disconnected from this holiness. What a marvel it was. What a comfort it offered. And what a contrary idea. What a threat to the way we humans are accustomed to living in the world.

Poet and essayist Alison Deming once wrote to me, "I don't think Americans know how to be reverent. Maybe the idea of revering anything means acknowledging its authority over us—a most undemocratic idea!" Her comment reminded me of William Sloane Coffin's acknowledgment in one of his essays of "the threat that authority always poses to power." Most of us are willing to acknowledge an authority greater than ourselves—indeed we often seek it out as a guiding principle for our lives. But we are inclined to give that authority a human likeness so that it can sanction our own sense of power. If such authority lies, instead, in the chemical language of a molecular structure that proves we have a fundamental bond to all other life on the planet, our conception of our own power begins to shift, to come into question. Perhaps that is why we, in Western cultures, have lived for centuries as though that bond did not exist. Perhaps that is why even something as compelling as the DNA discovery has not prompted us to give that bond the reverence it is due.

Our discomfort with this notion of a biological authority over our lives seems to be enough to keep us from taking the concept seriously. But what if we approached that essential truth from a different angle? What if we used a different metaphor? As Melinda Mueller was wrapping up her review lesson on DNA, she commented, "It is not a romantic notion to say that the earth is our home. Biologically, it is literally true." Home is not a place where we are uncomfortable. Home is a place that nurtures us, a place that reassures us of ourselves, a place to which we feel obligated, a place we are willing to protect, a place where relationships are fast and true. Home is a place where we know we belong. Home is a place infused with love.

In his book *The Land,* theologian and historian Walter Brueggemann recognizes a human yearning for place—for home—and acknowledges that yearning as a primary human hunger. I think of it as an instinctual desire and need for my own clearly defined habitat, a word primarily used to describe an ecological home range that allows a given species to thrive. We usually don't think of ourselves as the sample species, but I'd like to consider the notion of habitat in a human context for a moment. For those of us who use the English language, it is interesting to note that *habitat* is related to a cluster of other words—*habit, ability, rehabilitate, inhabit,* and *prohibit.* They all come from a common Latin root, *habere,* and spin off a fundamental concept of relationship: "to hold, hence to occupy or possess, hence to have." They constitute a family of words that ground us by describing where we live, how we live, what we are able to do, how we heal ourselves, what our connections are to the landscape around us, what the boundaries are for our behavior. Together, they offer a set of parameters that might allow us to thrive in a place we think of as home.

Given the biological evidence that the earth is our home, it's not difficult or even particularly imaginative to assert that we in Western societies have been living for centuries in a perpetual state of homesickness. We have worked hard—somewhat blindly and somewhat successfully—to disconnect ourselves from the source of our being. Our efforts have only partially succeeded because we cannot, in fact, separate ourselves from the fundamental truth of the context for our lives. For all those centuries we were not in a position to see and clearly understand the evidence, but science—one of the very tools that has given us the knowledge and capability of disengaging ourselves—has pointed us right back to where we belong.

One of the ironies of the human endeavor of science is that it rests on a foundation of objectivity and rational thought. It allows no room in its method for the emotions that are so fundamental to the human condition. The scientific evidence offered by the DNA discovery didn't exactly elicit a response of love, and yet it strikes me that such a reaction may be exactly right. Our legacy of homesickness stems in part from our inability to love the biological facts of our lives. The human hunger for place that Brueggemann speaks of might be thought of as a longing to be reconnected to the very source of our being. That longing is also a hunger for love—for the nurturing that a home place provides, for its familiarity, its comfort, its human community, its natural community, its light and landscape. I believe, too, that our hunger for place is a yearning for a sense of the holy, for home ground sacred

enough to sustain our faith, sacred enough that we will
not violate it, sacred enough that our commitment to its
holiness will not falter.

A spirited gospel hymn I learned when I was growing
up still rings in my memory. The first verse goes like this:

> This world is not my home, I'm just a-passing through
> My treasures are laid up somewhere beyond the blue
> The angels beckon me from heaven's open door
> And I can't feel at home in this world anymore.

The hymn was part of the indoctrination that had me believing for too many years that it wasn't worth my while
to attach myself to any particular place on Earth and that
the sacred did not exist here. Only when my heart defied
the first notion did the second prove itself untrue. Only
when I opened myself, as a Taoist scholar has said, to the
scripture of the landscape did the sacredness of Earth's
life become apparent. Only when I followed my own
calling to a particular place did I begin to ground myself
in that larger context—human and other—that contains
my life. And it has been here, in the place that is now my
home, that I have come to understand the strength of
love.

I don't find it difficult to move from my heart's ties to
the water-bound forested mountains of Baranof Island
to a sense of loyalty to that landscape and place. And it
is not much of a stretch for that loyalty to develop into
a covenant, an agreement that I live well in this place in
exchange for my respect and regard for the natural communities that surround and support me as well as the

shared human community. Brueggemann speaks of the yearning for place as a decision to enter history. I opted to join the local Sitka story at a point well along in its evolution. The Tlingit people had inhabited the place for millennia in the company of hemlock and cedar, salmonberry and skunk cabbage, brown bear and black-tailed deer, sea lion and orca, sockeye and halibut, raven and chickadee. My European predecessors, arriving some two hundred years ago, found a landscape largely undisturbed by human occupation. They and the many who have come after did not leave it as they found it. In places the landscape is irrevocably altered. Still, it offers itself as an extraordinary conjunction of forest and mountain and ocean that is home to every species that existed when Westerners first arrived. The Tlingit are still here too.

In its more recent history, Sitka was thought of as a timber town, with fishing and tourist-flooded streets in summer providing secondary sources of revenue. A Japanese-owned pulp mill was the unassailable mainstay of the economy for thirty years, with timber-harvesting privileges that were the envy of the industry outside Alaska. The related environmental controversies couldn't have been wished on anybody. They pitted neighbor against neighbor and created a deep festering wound in the community. The day the management broke the news that the mill was going to close its doors, people stood by radio speakers in homes and businesses all over town, listening in stunned silence. Some later celebrated, others grieved. Everyone wondered what would happen next.

I had lived for years with the tea brown water in the bay beyond my windows. I had walked outside into sulfured air on the many days when the wind carried the mill's emissions toward town. I was not going to be sorry to see those things go. But the scale of the change for the community made me uneasy. What, indeed, would happen next? Would people's worst fears come true? Without the mill as its economic backbone, would the community be diminished beyond repair? Would Sitka remain a town where I could live?

In the years since the mill closure, I have threaded my way in and around the social and economic challenges that have faced this small island community. I've listened to voices of fear and anger, satisfaction and hope. I've watched the change: some families have left town, others have moved in; property values and new home construction have climbed; a regional Native hospital has taken the economic lead; new small businesses have both failed and succeeded, several old businesses are thriving. I've listened to people slowly let go of the past and imagine a different future. And I've made it my work to collaborate with others to encourage the community to face some of its hardest questions: How can we delineate those parameters that will allow us to thrive here? How can we reassure ourselves that we will be able to live well on into the future? How can we create a stable economy? How can we make use of the natural resources around us without abusing them? What can we do to keep people—young and old—from being disillusioned about their lives? How can we make sure there is adequate affordable housing for all who live here? What can we do about racism? About equity? How can we improve on the ways we resolve our differences? After years of divisiveness on a variety of public issues, how can we learn to trust one another?

What has become apparent in this period of community transition is that one of the things that binds together people of almost all persuasions is their love of this place. I find it remarkable that we don't use that common ground more often to heal ourselves, for such love of place is as strong a bond as most any that can be found. Essayist Kathleen Dean Moore noted recently how quickly our obligation to a place and its human community follows on the heels of our love for the land and for each other. Our commitment begins with the fact of our love. And the health of a human community—economic, social, spiritual—is sustained first and foremost by the shared commitment and engagement of its citizens. If we expect to live well in this place, expect it to support us, expect it to be the source of what we need for both vocation and avocation, I believe we are obliged to acknowledge not only our responsibilities to each other, but the deeper connection—the holy connection—we share with the rest of life here. If the stands of spruce and hemlock and cedar gracing a secluded mountain-rimmed bay fill us with a quiet joy, if the silver flash of a salmon on the end of our line delights us, if the breach of a humpback whale thrills and silences us, if the first spring thrush song gladdens us, we can do no better than to return the love we've found. We can do no better than to live our lives—

individually and in community—as though all those living things mattered.

When I returned to the haven of our snowbound house, I listened as I approached and could hear the chirping bird chorus coming from the front porch. I walked quietly along the back side to a corner where I could sneak a look without disturbing them. They were busy. Juncos fluttered at the feeder perches not occupied by pine siskins. Chickadees ducked in and out, grabbing a sunflower seed and flying off with it into the trees. Thrushes hopped along the edge of the porch picking up whatever had fallen. Sparrows scratched methodically at the snow to uncover yesterday's seeds. I smiled. When I moved around the corner, they whirred away to the safety of surrounding bushes and branches. As soon as I got inside and closed the door, they returned. I settled down to watch. The day's light was fading. It had softened the whiteness of the snow. The clouds above the mountains across the bay were tinged a rosy gray. The birds took advantage of every moment of light, scurrying about, fortifying themselves against the coming hours of cold darkness. The water beyond them seemed to move in a steady easy current as a slight breeze riffled its surface. That breath of wind caught the cedar boughs hanging in front of the house and slipped on by. As it did, the corner of my eye caught a motion. A few thrush feathers fluttered where they were stuck on the window. I went out, gathered them up, and brought them inside. They were soft and almost silky, weightless in my hand. At their base they were downy and fluffy and a gentle blue gray. Midway up the shaft they gained a flatter rounded shape and turned burnt orange. And against that orange, the end of each feather was tipped in black. Feather upon feather, they had been layered to create first warmth, then the distinctive contour and color of that thrush's breast, then the dark necklace stripe around his neck. I savored their miracle, their particularity and purpose, and put them in a small birch-bark box where I will keep them as reminders of the sacred bond that underlies our lives.

Benediction

I was six years old, sitting on the hard wooden pew in the Vengurla church, my head in my mother's lap. She was gently stroking my hair back around my ear, easing me through the last parts of the Sunday service. I had tried to be earnest in my presence there, but couldn't grasp the meanings of all the Marathi words in Reverend Vasantrao Rambhise's sermon. I occupied myself with a miniature book, one I paged through often during these Sunday mornings. Its pastel floral borders and illustrations charmed me. I don't remember any of the words. But the book wasn't long enough to fill up the time. I fidgeted impatiently and finally laid my head down. My mother's thigh was comfortable under my cheek, the fabric of her dress smooth and cool. The fans circling overhead spread an easy breeze down over the congregation and I felt it on my bare arms and my heat-damp neck. Vasantrao's voice was reassuring and kind. Though I couldn't see him, I could almost hear his easy smile in the words he spoke. At last he invoked the final prayer and I closed my eyes and listened, waiting.

   . . . *Amen.*

John Gordpode, the blind organist, played the soft first chord of the benediction hymn and the congregation began to sing quietly. I added my small voice to the choir of others, my head still down in my mother's lap.

Krista, pavitra, shanti, satpriti ti;
Shoba, sownderya, maziya jivani.
Yeshu pavitra tu,
Shudha maza kari—
Thuzhay sownderya diso ya jivani.

The words described the holy peace of Christ's being, the beauty and purity of that holiness, the longing to find such beauty and peace within oneself. I sang them unknowingly. The gentle melody floated on the warm air, wrapped itself in the filigreed light that streamed in through the wooden scrollworked cross set into the church wall behind the altar. I basked in that comfort and wished it would last and last. Our hushed voices sang into a stillness that lingered at the end of each line, that hung on the final note. We sat a few moments in the blessed silence. Then pews began to creak and sandals shuffled as people got up and walked outside into the bright heat of the tropical sun.

In June, the week of summer solstice, that time of year when the light stays on and on, my parents came to Sitka for the annual symposium I organize, a week that is one of the highlights of my year. The symposium gathers fifty remarkable people to synthesize word and idea, story and concept, poem and conviction. My father, first, and then my mother, had become believers, keeping their distance in the program's early years, but then opening themselves to the symposium's engagement of heart and mind. This was the fourth time they had both attended. We had all thought hard, wrapped ourselves around the year's thematic questions about ways of seeing and ways of knowing. We had puzzled and laughed, explored perspectives we liked and didn't, considered notions that took us deeper into ourselves. And we had bid our farewells to all who had nourished our spirits during that all too uncommon gathering of inquisitive and respectful minds.

My parents were staying on a few extra days, sharing the house with Dorik and me. Our haven in the forest on the edge of Thimbleberry Bay offered just the right regimen after the symposium's intensity—quiet, unscheduled time to sleep late, read, sit at the window, share both silence and words. The water and its surrounding mountains and light let our minds roam. Ravens and fish crows and herons came and went. Occasionally a harbor seal would stretch its nose into the air, then look around watchfully. Our congregation of winter ducks was gone. The sun stayed high in the sky. The air was pleasantly cool. The forest stood by with its steadfast presence. We eased through those days and into the later hours of simple dinners and wine.

One of those evenings, after we had gone to bed, I lay upstairs next to Dorik, listening to the day's end. Downstairs, from the futon my parents shared in our living room, I could hear my father praying. I recognized the reverent tone in his voice, the cadences I had become accustomed to as a child, and tuned my ear more closely as he opened his heart to both my mother and to God. He was praying for his children—one by one—each of us named and blessed, each of our loved ones added to the list, husbands and wives and grandchildren, all given to the capacious and caring hand of God, all bestowed with love.

Outside the window, in the slowly fading light, a hermit thrush sang from a nearby tree. His fluted voice spilled his melody through the cool air, repeating it again and again, each first note crystalline, each refrain liquid and clear, each cascading sequence a heavenly accompaniment to my father's prayer. I lay still and closed my eyes, grateful for those holy blessings.

Acknowledgments

The essays in this book were written over a period of ten years. A few of them first appeared in other publications: "Soundings" in *North Dakota Quarterly;* "Of Landscape and Longing" in a different form in *Petroglyph;* "Cobb Island" in *Alaska Quarterly Review;* and "Thoughts on Trees: Who Could Live Without This Grace?" in *Great River Review.* My thanks to each of those journals.

Were it not for the annual Sitka Symposium, I would not have had the opportunity to meet a great many of the people who nourished these essays. That program and the several hundred people who have attended it over the years served as a wellspring for much of the material in this book. I would like to acknowledge particular thanks to John Hildebrand, Bill Kittredge, Barry Lopez, Tom Lyon, Melinda Mueller, Chet Raymo, Scott Sanders, and Terry Tempest Williams.

Other friends, colleagues, and mentors also nurtured this work, some with comments, some with encouragement, some by example. My thanks go to Ted Chamberlin, Lauren Davis, Alison Deming, Gary Holthaus, Sandra

Lopez, Valerie Miner, Kathy Moore, Joanne Mulcahy, Migael Scherer, Jeb Sharp, Pete Sinclair, and Don Snow.

Sitka fellow writers and friends Caroline Goodwin, Tina Johnson, Yvonne Mozeé, Richard Nelson, Shawn Newell, and John Straley each played a part in this book's coming into being, as did Old Harbor Books and long-time colleagues Don Muller and Marylin Newman.

Jim Kilgo and Nan Peacocke each taught me important lessons about faith in the work. My thanks. I am also grateful for two residencies at Hedgebrook—grateful to Nancy Nordhoff for her vision in creating such an extraordinary retreat for women writers, grateful to the Hedgebrook staff for their exceptional care.

My family's help in reviving and verifying childhood memories was invaluable. Special gratitude goes to Les and Harriet Servid, Leslie Williams, Laura Servid, and Mark Servid. And to Irikini Fernandez, for those early years of care and acceptance.

I'm indebted to Emilie Buchwald, editor and publisher at Milkweed Editions, for her keen literary sensibilities that strengthened this collection.

And for unbounded support, faith, and love, thanks beyond words to Dorik Mechau.

Works Cited

p. 14   Pattiann Rogers, "The Determinations of the
        Scene" in *Firekeeper: New and Selected Poems*
        (Minneapolis: Milkweed Editions, 1994), 32–33.

p. 18   Walter Brueggemann, "Land as Promise and as
        Problem" in *The Land* (Philadelphia: Fortress
        Press, 1977), 4.

p. 39   Robert Hass, "Meditation at Lagunitas" in *Praise*
        (New York: The Ecco Press, 1979), 4–5.

p. 80   Ezra Pound, "LIX" in *The Cantos* (New York:
        New Directions, 1956), 70.

p. 83   T. S. Eliot, "Little Gidding" in *Four Quartets*
        (New York: Harcourt Brace and Company, 1970),
        59. Copyright © 1942 by T. S. Eliot and renewed
        1970 by Esme Valerie Eliot. Reprinted with per-
        mission from Harcourt, Inc.

p. 102 Mally Strong, "Finding Words." Copyright © 2000
        by Mally Strong. Reprinted with permission from
        the author.

p. 147 Philip Levine, "Snow" in *New Selected Poems*
        (New York: Knopf, 1991), 192. Copyright © 1991
        by Philip Levine. Reprinted with permission

from Alfred A. Knopf, a division of Random House Inc.

p. 155   Wendell Berry, *Harlan Hubbard: Life and Work* (New York: Pantheon Books, 1990), 33.

p. 156   Harlan Hubbard, quoted in Wendell Berry, *Harlan Hubbard: Life and Work* (New York: Pantheon Books, 1990), 33.

p. 167   Harlan Hubbard, quoted in Wendell Berry, *Harlan Hubbard: Life and Work,* 34.

p. 168   Robert Frost, "Birches" in *The Poetry of Robert Frost,* edited by Edward Connery Lathem (New York: Holt, Rinehart and Winston, 1969), 122.

p. 174   William Sloane Coffin, "Authority, Not Power" in *Living the Truth in a World of Illusions* (San Francisco: Harper and Row, 1985), 5.

I'm grateful to *Wooden Boat* magazine and the *Lowell's Boat Shop Newsletter* for historical information about Lowell's Boat Shop. I'd also like to acknowledge James V. Powell's chapter on the Quileute Indians in the *Handbook of North American Indians,* vol. 7, and Kenneth Owens and Alton Donnelly's book, *The Wreck of St. Nikolai.* Both provided valuable information about the Quileute, their traditions and territories, and their first encounters with Western culture. And thanks to Mally Strong for permission to include her poem, "Finding Words."

CAROLYN SERVID has lived in Sitka, Alaska, since 1980. She is a cofounder of The Island Institute, a nonprofit organization whose aim is to encourage people to think creatively about how best to live together in community and place. She and her husband are currently codirectors of the organization. She is editor of two anthologies, *From the Island's Edge: A Sitka Reader* (Graywolf, 1995), a collection of poetry and prose by participants in the Institute's annual Sitka Symposium, and, with Donald Snow, *The Book of the Tongass* (Milkweed, 1999).

More Books on The World As Home
from Milkweed Editions

To order books or for more information, contact
Milkweed at (800) 520-6455
or visit our website (www.milkweed.org).

Brown Dog of the Yaak:
Essays on Art and Activism
Rick Bass

Boundary Waters:
The Grace of the Wild
Paul Gruchow

Grass Roots:
The Universe of Home
Paul Gruchow

The Necessity of Empty Places
Paul Gruchow

A Sense of the Morning:
Field Notes of a Born Observer
David Brendan Hopes

Taking Care:
Thoughts on Storytelling and Belief
William Kittredge

The Barn at the End of the World:
The Apprenticeship of a Quaker, Buddhist Shepherd
Mary Rose O'Reilley

Walking the High Ridge:
Life As Field Trip
Robert Michael Pyle

Ecology of a Cracker Childhood
Janisse Ray

The Dream of the Marsh Wren:
Writing As Reciprocal Creation
Pattiann Rogers

The Country of Language
Scott Russell Sanders

The Book of the Tongass
Edited by Carolyn Servid and Donald Snow

Homestead
Annick Smith

Testimony:
Writers of the West Speak On Behalf of Utah Wilderness
Compiled by Stephen Trimble and Terry Tempest Williams

Shaped by Wind and Water:
Reflections of a Naturalist
Ann Zwinger

Other books of interest to
The World As Home reader:

ANTHOLOGIES

Sacred Ground:
Writings about Home
Edited by Barbara Bonner

Urban Nature:
Poems about Wildlife in the City
Edited by Laure-Anne Bosselaar

Verse and Universe:
Poems about Science and Mathematics
Edited by Kurt Brown

POETRY

Boxelder Bug Variations
Bill Holm

Butterfly Effect
Harry Humes

Eating Bread and Honey
Pattiann Rogers

Firekeeper:
New and Selected Poems
Pattiann Rogers

Interior design by Donna Burch
Typeset in Joanna, New Baskerville, and Apollo
by Stanton Publication Services, Inc.
Printed on acid-free 55# Phoenix Opaque Natural paper
by Edwards Brothers